The Horny Heart?

By

Paula Jacobsson

-Is Love really the answer to everything?

everything?

-YES!

TABLE OF CONTENT

Consultation with God

-God I need your help! I want to write a book on sex, porn and love and I'm not quite sure how to go about it....Halloooooo! Do you hear me?

-Hrrm, yeah, yes I heard you, what do you need me for?

-Well, these are not entirely straight forward subjects to write about without things coming out the wrong way, I mean, people have so many thoughts and opinions on each and every one of them and they stir up so many different emotions. I want it to be a book that people can read and feel inspired by. I mean inspired towards consciousness and joy when it comes to sex and love. So many seem to have so many problems with it today and from my perspective sex and love are two of the best things in life – almost the meaning of life.

-Sex and love – the meaning of life? Yes, well, why not, they are both creative forces and I have to say that in the area of creativity and creating I am somewhat of an expert.

-Yes, haha, exactly, but at the same time we sometimes make it so difficult and complicated that we feel paralyzed by the whole thing, I mean we do actually have sex more frequently for completely different reasons than creating new life.

-Yes...hrmm...well, I have noticed.

-Do you think that's wrong?

-Absolutely not, you have bodies that are supposed to give you lots and lots of joyful experiences, as long as you cooperate with your heart and soul that is.

-Exactly, but sex for the sake of sex, what is your opinion on that?

-Sex just for the sake of sex doesn't exist. You always have sex for a reason, just because you are not aware of it doesn't mean that you have sex for the sake of sex. And no, I don't mean that you only should have sex to start a family, even if that is fantastic as well.

-OK, this is exactly what I feel could be difficult to communicate, because some people, or quite a few really, don't see the context, they think that sex is something separate that you can get involved in, sort of like a hobby.

-Hahaha, ok I see what you mean, but if you think about it there is no such thing as just having a hobby for the sake of the hobby either.

-Eh, do you think you could elaborate on that?

-This is what I mean; even if you have, let's say golf as a hobby, you spend your time golfing not just to do it, you are interested and into golf for several reasons It could be that it gives you satisfaction when you improve at the game, the joy you get from spending time with your golfing buddies, the connectedness you experience from belonging to a certain golf club, the confidence it gives you when you have a good score, the freedom you feel when you're outdoors, the excitement over the possibility to do a hole in one, the pride you feel over your expensive equipment, the prestige it gives you to be involved in an exclusive sport, the distraction it generates from work, home, or whatever it might be… do you want me to continue?

-No, I think you've made your point, hmmm, this is one of the reasons these subjects can be quite a challenge to write about.

-Yes I agree, if you want to write about everything regarding sex, porn and love you'll most likely write for a very long time before you're finished, if you ever will be. You know I am the only one who really knows EVERYTHING.....don't you think it suffices if you write down your own thoughts about it all?

-Yes, that's the way it'll have to be, I have thought about it a lot, been thru a lot and have a lot of opinions and ideas about it.

-Sooooo, what are you waiting for?

SEX, PORN AND LOVE!

As I came home he came to meet me in the doorway, dressed in a white silk shirt, worn out jeans and a kitchen towel stuffed into the pocket of his pants. He drew me close and kissed me on the cheek, put his arm around my waist and let the other softly caress my right breast. I felt the stirring of a few butterflies in my tummy.

–I want to take a shower so that I can rinse off the day, I said and smiled. He took a step back, grabbed me by the hand and pulled me out to the kitchen.

–A drink before the shower? He had made me a Vodka Martini, my favourite.

–I'll take it with me into the bathroom. I took a sip and enjoyed the cold fluid, put the glass down carefully by the sink and took off my clothes. When the warm water ran over my body I felt the stress and boredom of yet another day at work leave me. I let the water continue to run over my body as I let my thoughts return to the moment when he had grazed my breast. The excitement stirred again and I felt slightly impatient with expectation. I put a towel around my wet hair and put lotion on my body to make it soft and scented. A splash of perfume on the neck and between the breasts and then some mascara and rouge. I left my hair to dry by itself, it looked good enough. I brought the almost finished drink with me to the kitchen.

-Wow, hey beautiful, he said and smiled that lovely smile. He pulled me close again and let his hands touch my back and my hips. He made a quick manoeuvre and was behind me in an instant with his arms around me. I saw how he with a swift movement put his finger in one of the pots on the stove, dipped his finger in the sauce and then let me taste it. He let his finger stay in my mouth and slowly moved it back and forth. He turned towards me again and touched my lips with his fingers; he touched my face, my neck. He looked intensely into my eyes and we both drew a deep breath as if preparing for the wave of feelings we knew would be the result of us giving in to desire and kiss. Slowly, very slowly, we moved closer together and finally let our lips meet, just for a short moment. He then started kissing me all over my face as if he wanted to prolong this moment of expectation for as long as possible. He came closer to my lips again and I felt my whole being wanting him to kiss me senseless, but he hesitated yet another moment and took my face into his hands and looked at me as if I was the eighth wonder of the world.

He smiled, mostly with his eyes and he came closer so slowly that I wasn't sure he was moving at all, and finally let me have his mouth completely. The warmth from his lips spread down throughout my body and I gave into the passion, I just wanted to give myself over to it, not think, just be in that feeling, devour him and lose myself in it until all that remained of me was lust. He stopped for a short moment, looked into my eyes and pulled back a little, still looking into my eyes. We smiled at each other, that beautiful kind of smile and fleeting

moment of reality check before we once again allowed our passion to run its course until we both lay sweating, exhausted and panting, wrapped around each other in the now moist sheet as if we had just barely managed to escape from a looming disaster.

♥

SEX – an instinctive force of nature that gives life and is life

I just Googled the word "sex", and I got no less than *one billion one hundred seventy million hits*. More than one billion hits, that's pretty impressive. What does that tell us? Are most of us a bunch of sex maniacs? Well, I haven't really investigated all other search criteria but it implies a few things. It's obvious that a lot of us search for sex or for information about sex on the internet. We think about sex, we have problems with sex, we reflect over sex, we want to know more about sex, we enjoy sex, we worry about sex – sex interests us in so many ways and on so many levels. Sex is one of our more basic needs and maybe it's not that surprising that with today's technology sex is one of the most intensely searched for subjects on the net. But, sex on the internet includes a lot more than just plain sex. The search generates a lot of sites with porn, not so surprising, sites concerning relationships, about diseases and a lot of other stuff as well. But, in my perspective sex isn't the equivalent to porn, it's something completely different.

SEX AND REPRODUCTION

They had come to a decision, they had been together long enough, they knew each other, they loved each other and wanted, as far as they could tell right now, be with each other for the rest of their lives. They had a very satisfying relationship, they enjoyed each other's company, they were each other's best friends and they had also been able to keep the passion and chemistry alive. Up until now they had used birth control but she had for a period of time now felt it to be unsatisfactory to know that she couldn't or wouldn't become pregnant. She hadn't talked about it, just been somewhat bewildered with her own thoughts and feelings about it. She hadn't really thought of herself as a woman who wanted kids now, some day in the future perhaps, but not now.

He too had been surprised by his reaction at that time when she had told him she had forgotten to take her pill. His desire had been so much stronger, something inside him, even if he wasn't sure how to express it, had felt as if he had wanted this last barrier between them to open. He wasn't sure if it was as simple as him wanting to see if they did become pregnant, but he didn't think so, it had felt more compelling and instinctive. Months later he had, in a joking tone suggested that she quit the pill since it didn't give a hundred percent protection anyway and that it did constitute a bit of a health hazard. None of them realized that this, somewhat casually uttered comment was what would make them discuss the matter seriously. It hadn't been long after that that they agreed that a baby would be ok and that they looked forward to experiencing this together. They realized that this gave them a completely new dimension to their relationship, on how they viewed each other, now as possible parents in the making. The day had come when her body had gone back to its natural state and she was no longer "protected". They had had a night out, eating at their favourite restaurant and they had talked about how it felt that they now could actually become pregnant. The atmosphere between them had filled with a new kind of respect and in a way it was as if they now realised the reality of their decision. A little like when two kids for the first time do something that feels really grown up and almost a bit forbidden

When they came home, they watched TV for a while, each sipping a glass of wine, enjoying a nice movie He turned to look at her now and then and felt he saw her with completely different eyes. He wasn't sure what it was, but tonight she was more beautiful than ever, her eyes, her lips, her hair, breasts, her long legs that were stretched out before her. He took her hand and she turned towards him and smiled. He caressed her hand, trailed her veins with his forefinger, turned her palm upwards and kissed it. They both felt the familiar desire awaken and she moved so that she sat on his lap facing him. They kissed softly for a long while; they looked at each other while peeling off their clothes. She felt such an overwhelming rush of tenderness when she looked at him, she wanted to take him in her arms and hold him like that as if to protect him from all harm. He felt an almost magical mix of love, tenderness, protectiveness and power that made it hard for him to control his desire to enter her and stay there until the end of time. When she straddled him and let him in, deeply and slowly, their emotions moved them both to tears. This time everything felt different, he moved inside her and the knowledge that they now, for the first time, were completely "naked", without any obstacles in the way made his desire grow even stronger She felt open and vulnerable and safe and powerful at the same time and wanted everything he had to give with both her body and her heart. They couldn't stop gazing into each other's eyes and what they saw mirrored the unexpected awe, love and new depth of closeness they both felt, which so beautifully blended with the pure physical lust that drove them on. When they climaxed they both experienced a short moment of dissolving into each other, a moment they both knew they would cherish and keep in their hearts for the rest of their lives

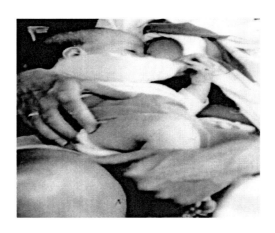

♥

We have received our sex drive to reproduce, to keep mankind as a race on the planet. If we had been devoid of sex drive, neither you, nor me would be here, man would be extinct before she even existed sort of. Our sex drive is an instinctive force, a need that sometimes feels just as compelling as hunger and thirst. We can live without sex, but that's not to be recommended. We have our sex drive and it is a necessity to protect the human race, to protect life's continuation and it is important that we understand that fact. It is natural to have a sex drive, we all have it, from the day we are born until the day we die, provided we don't during the course of our lives at some point are hurt or damaged in some way that destroys it. When our sex drive is at its healthiest we can enjoy it however it shows up, that is, very intensely at times and not so intensely at other.

However, our society isn't really created for instinctive human needs and we can't, as free creatures in nature, engage in sexual activities whenever and wherever we feel like it.

We no longer just have sex to reproduce either. Truth be told, my guess is that it's only a fraction of the total amount of time spent on sex that we have it to have kids. Yes, many of us do it to have kids, but even those who want kids also have sex "just for the fun of it". Some have sex just to pass time, some to release stress, some as a hobby, some as a necessary evil, some are addicted, some see sex as a science that should be explored and analyzed and yet others use it as a tool for spiritual development. We are all different and as long as we are aware of what we are doing, why and most importantly what kind of force we are dealing with, it's ok. But today there are not many who fully realize neither what their sex drive entails nor how to handle it to make the most of it.

A lot of activities start in our bodies when the sex drive is turned on. Certain hormones are produced and distributed, muscles contract or expand, blood is drawn to certain places, we secrete scents and fluids or just simply put - a body in lust is like a carnival of happenings. Lust as a mere physical sensation feels more like some sort of itchiness, like when we have a small rash that we want to scratch and not like a deep need that feels like a matter of life and death. That kind of itch is not what I'm referring to when I talk about our instinctive sex drive which is complex and includes the need for both physical and emotional stimuli in a perfect mix. In the former scenario it's a sensation that is very limited and more often than not localised strictly in our genitals and in the latter it's a matter of a longing, a need that is felt on all levels. The first can be stilled in less than a minute, but even then it doesn't suffice with just physical stimulation. Physical stimulation or touch doesn't quench or cause desire by itself. Most of us has experienced a situation where we're just not turned on by our partner's touch, we are distracted, feel off somehow or whatever else and most likely we have noticed that no matter how much effort he or she puts into it, nothing much happens - except maybe that we feel a chafe coming on.

So much has been written on all the taboos that have to do with sex and how inhibiting they can be. We have been warned about "the lust of the flesh" both by the guardians of morality as well as by religious fanatics and fools. Always with the warning that if we give in to this lust we are about to make a huge mistake and will be lost. On the one hand I can agree, but with the proviso that those who give in to the lust of the flesh without seeing themselves as whole and complex beings and take that into consideration do risk to lose both themselves and their footing, while on the other hand those who deeply understand their own sexuality and the sex drive as a force have nothing to lose and everything to gain by giving in and enjoying it thoroughly.

For me personally sex has not always been free from taboos, absolutely not, I as so many others of my generation grew up thinking that sex was something you did in the dark, it was secret and you really only did it because you had to in order to have babies. I remember how my friends told me that my parents were bad since they had "done it" at least three times (we are three siblings) and those friends who were single children or only two siblings felt proud that their parents hadn't done it as many times. I couldn't really understand how my parents could be viewed as bad in that area, they were incredibly embarrassed by the subject and the whole thing was pretty confusing for me. But, I did spend a few of my childhood years thinking that sex was something you just had to do if you wanted kids, no matter how disgusting the whole concept of it was.

To be able to connect the sex that grownups had to have in order to have kids with the feelings I could be swept up by at night when I'd gone to bed, didn't even occur to me. I had a feeling that it wasn't really ok to feel the way I did, but at the same time there wasn't that much to do about it. It felt good and besides I was the only one who noticed anyway. When I became a little older and understood the connection I felt somewhat guilt ridden and worried for a while, but that passed with time and more knowledge.

Many experience their first sexual encounter as confusing, exciting and a bit fumbled. Not everybody have sex the first time because they are so utterly taken by desire that they just can't help themselves. Some have sex because they want to know what it's all about, some because they think they have to, some because they think that everybody else has done it, and some lucky ones do it because they are in love and feel that it is a natural next step after the kissing and hugging.

I was the one who waited the longest among my peers and was the last one who "did it" just because I finally didn't want to wait any longer. I had been afraid that it would be painful and I almost looked at it as going to the dentist to fix a cavity. The entire adventure was over after less than a minute and I couldn't help laughing afterwards. Not a short chuckle of a laugh either, a full blown explosion that almost ripped my sides apart. It was most likely the excitement and pent up tension being released and I do understand that the guy must have felt miserable even if I did my best to explain that it wasn't his performance that made me laugh.

My first "real" relationship where sex was involved surprised me. I discovered that I became excited in a whole new way, it wasn't just the stirring in my groin, it was an excitement that included so much more. Despite the fact that he never managed to get me to orgasm, neither one of us were very experienced or skilled, I did find sex completely fascinating. I loved to kiss, touch and just feel the desire grow until I felt I completely turned into passion from head to toe. And even though I wasn't sure what it was I wanted, I knew I wanted more, more of the intoxicating emotions and more of the gratifying feeling it gave me to try and discover how I could make him lose it completely by exciting him as much as I possibly could.

Now, when I have achieved what you could call "maturity" I have tried a few things more and have several experiences that has given me a fuller view of sex. With a fuller view I

20

mean the experiences I have had with different men and the different compositions of feelings I have had for these men as well as my own sex drive at different occasions. Sexual desire and the sex drive as such are so much more complex than it was then, when I first discovered it. Now it can resemble what is often called a religious experience and I feel a deep respect for my sexual desire since it, in my universe, symbolizes the very force of life.

Let's go back to the sex drive as a need for reproduction. As a woman I have to admit that it is pretty amazing how the sex drive can tenfold when I ovulate. It took me a while to see the connection, at first I just found it almost tedious to occasionally feel like a "bitch in heat". Because even if you do know how to satisfy yourself, it was a man I wanted…and as life would have it, it hasn't always been that one has been around, but when there was…..:)

There's something insatiable in the sex drive that is awake during ovulation, you can feel satisfied after having sex with a partner you like but the interval between the re-charges is so much shorter which makes you want it that more often than during the rest of the menstrual cycle. In these moments I can feel insatiable, it's like drinking and drinking and still being thirsty, but in a very pleasant way.

When it dawned on me that I, or my body, wanted to reproduce and signalled this very clearly I felt a new respect for the intelligence inherent in it and also for the very sensation of sexual desire. It became so much more than just a physical sensation, I experienced it as something basic almost animalistic. Now I know that not all of us feel comfortable giving in to the animal or "beast" inside, but for me, who's always loved animals and who has never viewed mankind as something truly exceptional, (maybe apart from our thinking and reflecting capacity), there is no problem at all to acknowledge the instinctive aspects. It feels fantastic, grand and true.

It's not that I have wanted to make a baby every time I have ovulated, I have one kid and that is great, but to feel and give in to the power of this sexual desire that is fed both by this ancient and inbred force as well as the pure pleasure of it, is a blessing. It gives us a greater understanding of the needs and feelings our sex drive encompasses and also a wider perspective of the sex drive as a force in our lives. Our bodies are amazing and there are so many things we can do with them to enrich our lives with pleasurable experiences, and I do believe that what is at the top of the list for many of us, is to give ourselves extraordinary and breathtaking experiences that include both love and sex.

SEX AND PLAY

*What a week it had been. She had never worked this hard, early mornings and late nights. She had felt tired, irritated and worried as to whether everything would come out as planned. To plan this type of huge events was incredibly stressful. She knew she had taken out a lot of it on Patrick, but she became even more annoyed when she came home all worked out and he sat there, watching TV with a take away bag from McDonalds at his side. Never that he thought about the fact that she might be hungry when she came home or that she wanted him to take care of her a bit, think about buying home breakfast foods for the next morning or even something simple as to run her a bath. Yesterday they had argued and she had complained about what an egotistical jerk he was who **never** did anything for her. She was aware that she was completely and utterly unfair saying those things but right now, when she was working so hard he could at least take on the routine chores of cooking, grocery shopping, vacuuming and doing the laundry. He had just looked at her, not reacted with anger at all just let her scream and shout. She felt he had been indifferent, as if he couldn't care any less, and that had irritated her even more. The argument had finished with her screaming at him that she too wanted to have an efficient wife so that she could focus on work and still count on dinner being cooked, clothes being washed and the house being clean and nice to come home to. She had slammed the bedroom door shut and hadn't awakened when he came to bed. The morning after she had still felt annoyed and she went* to work without awakening him. Now it was Friday night and she didn't want to fight any more even though she could still feel some of the anger. She was too tired to buy anything for dinner, or even a bottle of wine, she guessed she'd just have to settle for a cup of tea and a sandwich and he could eat whatever he wanted. When she stepped into the door she heard that he was playing music rather loudly and she could hear Mick Jagger's voice singing about Angie. He came hurrying towards her, in his robe, his hair standing on end as if he had been sleeping on his head. Only the small dim lights were turned on and she registered that she thought he looked somewhat strange, but had no time to think about it before he started to lecture her.

– Don't come in with your shoes on, I have vacuumed and I don't want to get sand all over the floor!. I hope you are hungry 'cause I have made dinner, which is now almost cold, you could have called to tell me you were late!

She could hear in his voice that he wasn't completely serious and that he was trying to mimic her. She drew a deep breath to respond that she wasn't in the mood for his sarcasms when she saw him turn around, turn the ceiling light on and with a theatrical gesture throw off *his robe. Underneath he had her knickers on, a garter belt and nylons, one of her frilly shirts, a pair of earrings and now when the lights were on she saw that he had put on eye shadow and lipstick and that his hair, that she had thought were just uncombed actually was his attempt at a do.*

She felt all her irritation run off her like melted ice and the laughter just burst out of her.

—You did say you wanted a wife, he said and his eyes twinkled when he walked towards her and took her in his arms. During dinner he kept her clothes on and when they were finished she wanted to try and make up his face with a bit more sophistication than he had managed. She took out her makeup bag and really put an effort into making his face up as well as she could, then she put on a larger pair of earrings and fixed his hair with mousse and hairspray. While she was busying herself with that he tried to kiss her and touch her wherever he got a chance to. When she was satisfied with her result she took him by the hand and led him into the bedroom where they had a full length mirror. She stood behind him so that he could see what she had accomplished. She started to caress him as if he really was a woman, her hands touched him in a completely different way than they used to, she came closer, kissed the back of his neck and put her hands on his buttocks as if she was going to take him from behind and then she gently removed her panties from his hips since they couldn't hide his excitement anyway. When he started to unbutton the garter belt in order to take off the stockings, she stopped him, smiled and asked him to keep them on….

♥

To maintain a sense of play during sex is something that makes it feel new no matter how old we get or how many times we've been thru it. I can almost hear everybody sighing and saying: "Yes, well that sounds great, but when you are tired after work, have kids to take care of, a home to maintain and about a thousand other duties and chores, there's not much playfulness nor sex drive left". I know that, I know how it feels to be so tired that all you can think of is the bed and the pillow and a good night's sleep. I had a time in my life when the only thing that got me out of bed in the morning was the thought that I could go to bed again later that night. Talk about rat race. In addition, the fact is that it's not uncommon that the desire and zest for sex doesn't show up simultaneously for both parties, when one is ON the other is OFF and vice versa which doesn't make it any easier.

The sexual desire can be disturbed by so many factors, we know that now after all the books that have been written on the subject, all the discussions, all the TV-shows, all relationship expert advices and so on and I'll come back to that a bit later when I talk about porn. Here and now I don't want to add any more to that than that it isn't all that easy to have a fabulous sex life with a partner, but it is possible, when we try not to complicate things further.

To retain a sense of playfulness is really important in any loving or healthily sexual relationship. We play more easily when we are relaxed and let go of thoughts of tomorrow, the bills we have to pay or other issues. The play, that is the willingness and ability to include something carefree and easygoing into our sexual activities gives us a completely different kind of experience than when we have sex as a stress release, a should or a deep need to connect with our partner. Sometimes the playfulness can create conditions that will renew or change our perspective in a way that gives us even more astounding sexual experiences.

It is beautiful to live with a partner who still likes to play, who surprises you with creative fun things that makes you laugh or at least smile and who keeps their childish sense of curiosity and exploration alive. To look at yourself and your partner as sources for enjoyment and leisure is only possible if you don't take everything too seriously. Seriousness often entails demands and requirements and those can be true pleasure-killers. Children play to develop, learn and have fun and we as adults don't need to stop doing that just because we

26

have lived a certain number of years. Instead of just expressing our sense of play within sports, hobbies and creative leisure activities we can let it enter the realm of our sex life, since that is the very place where it generates so much more than just a temporary thrill. We have our sex drive included in the package so to speak, and it would be a shame if we don't enjoy it since it is completely free of charge. Just because this is the case and because our sex drive in and of itself is a creative force, it is not suited to be tied down by too many rules, regulations, blockages and musts. When we let it roam, as it is, it grows and enriches our lives just as much as a real child does, which is its ultimate result in the physical world.

What I put in the word playfulness is not some kind of vision that we should all run around naked as children and play with our own or our partner's genitals all the time. It is more of a playfulness in how we look at ourselves and our sex lives. Some people live by routine and have certain days in the week, certain rituals that signal "now it's time for sex" and that may work for some. But to get some life into it it's important to dare to be spontaneous at times and trust those sparks of desire that can ignite even if it's not the right day of the week or the correct ritual has been performed. It's not necessary that sex always has to enclose all the components you feel are important or even last longer than ten seconds. Sometimes the little things suffice, like when I'm doing the dishes and he sneaks up behind me and hold his hands on my hips and pushes up against me for a brief moment before he returns to whatever he is doing, or that I, when he is sorting the laundry, pull down his pants and give his Willy a quick wet kiss, or when he caresses my breasts secretly so that the kids won't notice or I whisper something slightly naughty in his ear when he is speaking with his boss....it's like a perpetual flirt where we both are aware and attentive to each other as playmates and we know that these invites don't have to be something that needs to be followed up thoroughly at once and we keep our sense of humour when life on occasion doesn't offer any opportunities for long sexual explorations and in depth sessions.

The playfulness makes us aware that the possibility is right there, that we see and attract each other, that we safely can let the play remain play since we know that the sex drive and desire, when accepted and given space is limitless and continually refilled, and just because we know there's an endless supply of it, we can allow ourselves to play with it and within it. Our own intimate language and signals develop and give us a sense of connectedness that will spill over into all areas of our relationship. Play, per definition, means that there is a sense of laughter, a sense of humour and easy-goingness present. When kids play they don't care if they get dirty, messy or if the play involves tasting something that shouldn't be tasted, they just shrug it off and move on to the next adventure. Sex when it's good, has a resemblance to children's play, sex has to be allowed to be both sweaty, messy, wet, un-beautiful, noisy and even a bit ridiculous at times. Sex is too important to only be dealt with seriously, it's not until the seriousness is mixed with humour and play that it becomes refined and reaches its full potential, which by the way is something that is true for all areas of our lives, at least that's what I think.

We as humans have an opportunity to use play, give in to our desire or at times control it since we know it's always right there and we don't have to take it as a matter of life and death which it sometimes looks like when you look at wild animals and nature as a whole. The energy or the power which gives all baby animals their inbred drive to play is the same power that makes the black grouse dance and prance for his loved one, makes most of the male animals blow themselves up to a larger version of themselves to impress the female and even gets the salmon to swim upstream to spawn.

When you view your sex drive as a force of nature, it is even possible to feel a sort of excitement by nature itself, especially during spring. When I see everything waking up again after a long winter, with swelling buds, small newly born leaves that are light green and moist, colours and forms of all kinds I recognize the sex drive in all the re-creative, re-born, colourful and dazzling life that just explode out of former grey and seemingly dead branches and earth. In the same manner, my sex drive can make me feel new, colourful, creative, reborn and indomitable. I, we, as human beings have been given this possibility to play with this life force, with the basic creative energy and enjoy it in an ecstatic mixture of playfulness and deep seriousness which is a prerequisite for the experience we all dream of – paradise here on earth.

"If it's not fun, you're not doing it right." *Bob Basso*

SEX AND MUSIC

We had just arrived home from a concert with Simply Red and we were both exhilarated and almost felt high from the experience. There's always a special ambiance at great concerts and Simply Red's music made us both want to dance and feel good. When we had taken off our coats Daniel went out into the kitchen and put the kettle on and when it was done he returned to the living room with the cups and put them on the table. .

–We have to listen to some more music, or what do you say? He looked at me questioningly.

–Of course I said, since I wanted to keep this beautiful feeling going for a while longer. Daniel went over to the stereo and chose a CD. The music came on and we drank our tea, listened, talked a bit about the concert and re-lived a few of the high points. After a while Daniel changed Simply Red to a calmer and even more suggestive album.

–Come here, dance with me, Daniel looked at me, reached out his hand and smiled. He had had several years of dance education and moved his body like a god on any dance floor. I went over to him.

– You know I always feel a bit insecure when dancing with you, I said and made a face at him.

–Oh, stop it, I love it when you dance, come here let's do it like this. Daniel turned me around so that I had my back towards his stomach, he put his arms around me and we stood there for a while, just swaying slowly to the music. The lyrics were about lovemaking, sensual touching and groovy lovin'....I relaxed into his arms and let his body guide my movements. He had his hands on my hips and showed me how to move them from side to side together with him. I could feel his breath on my neck and it felt nice. The music had a distinct beat and I wanted to move with it.

–Listen, just listen and relax, Daniels voice in my ear felt almost hypnotic. I felt the length of his body against mine and because I had my back towards him it was easy to relax and follow his lead.

We stood there like two young trees in the wind and moved in exact sync. It was fantastic to feel his hands that now lay on my shoulders and slowly moved down towards my waist and as far down as he could reach down my legs. His lips touched my neck and I felt him lift a few strands of my hair so that he could kiss my naked skin. We stood like that for quite a while, slowly rocking, his lips kissing my neck from the shoulders all the way up to my *hairline. I could feel the music, the rhythm, the words as if I was listening with my entire body. I felt his hands starting to unbutton my blouse, button by button until he could take it off. He took off his t-shirt and now I felt his warm chest against my back. The bra was unbuttoned and his hands cupped my breasts as if to replace it. The warmth from his body and his hands did their magic and I could hear him breathing hard when he felt my breasts in his hands. We didn't speak, just kept on breathing and continued to move with the music.*

♥

I am very affected by music; it can change my mood in an instant. Some songs can make me feel sad and emotionally hungry, some make me feel energetic and excited and yet others speak to my sex drive. I know I'm not in any way unique, even science has now proved how much we are affected by music. Anyone who has been at the gym knows how much better the workout feels if you have good music in your headphones. What constitutes good music is on the other hand something where we differ enormously. What works for one can be a complete turn off to the other.

Music has always been a very important element in my life and now there are even people who claim that certain tones and certain types of music can heal people from a variety of diseases and blockages and I know that lots and lots of people use music to de-stress. Stress is one of the absolute most frequent reasons our emotions and feelings get ruffled and that of course includes the sex drive.

I have tried relaxation music during high stress periods of my life and for me it works. I have also used subliminal recordings and so called brain entrainment to release stress and stress symptoms. What I have discovered which I didn't expect was that my sex drive awakens by itself just from relaxing. As if it gets energized when the rest of my system relaxes without me having to do anything. I have to my surprise laid down to listen to a antistress CD and been as far away from sex thought wise as I could possibly be when I start listening just to notice how my thoughts and body become directed towards sex at the end of the recording. Not that I feel super excited or anything, I just notice the presence of the desire and lust when I am relaxed in a different way compared to when I'm involved with the daily stuff. That has made me realize even more how this force or power which can be so powerful and even compelling at times still backs down when I have problems or worries, so that I can focus on whatever needs to be done to solve them without it bothering me, and that makes me trust my desire and also trust that life is very wisely arranged for us.

Music as a source for inspiration is nothing new, but to really use it is far from most people's everyday reality. We listen to music casually and put on a record or the radio to have the distraction or just lift our spirits a bit. But for me music can be used as others use drugs, there are "uppers and downers" but with the added value of no side-effects (except for a possibly annoyed neighbour or a slight numbness in my ears).

The urge to dance and our sex drive are similar. Music makes us want to move our bodies and for most people the sex drive also makes us want to move our bodies ☺. That's not the only similarity; the urge to dance can feel almost as compelling as sexual urges when the right music is on. Still, not everybody dances, but most people start to move at least a foot or a hand to mark the rhythm. Music stimulates us and it's easy to tell when you play music for small children who can't even walk yet. Their bodies start to move in a rhythmical way and even if we as grownups look at them with critical eyes and find the movements only moderately dancelike, dancing is what the children are doing. As we grow up we learn to control these instinctual signals and we don't start to dance uncontrollably every time we hear a good piece of music, worried as we are to be perceived as crazy, ridiculous or something just as socially unacceptable. The expression coined by William Purkey: "Dance like nobody's watching" says a whole lot about how aware we are that we will be judged if we dance the way we feel like and that is similar to the number of opinions and views there are on what sex supposedly should look like to be deemed ok. So, here we could coin another expression: "Have sex like nobody's watching". Though that doesn't work as well since most of us want to have sex *with* someone and even if it can be fun to use a blindfold at times we usually want to be able to see our partner. What I'm after is more the feeling of complete abandonment and letting the music take you where it wants, without thoughts about how it looks or what is appropriate. The fear that music, or sex for that matter, will take us to the edge of insanity or at least that we will be perceived as balancing on the border, is highly exaggerated.

Try and see for yourself, dance, without looking at yourself in a mirror, just because you want to, don't think about how the movements may look, just feel them. The more you are able to relax and allow your body to move the way it wants to, the more tension is released and the more the fear diminishes and you will realize that you won't die of shame or anything else, you will most likely feel more alive than before you started. The more we dance the more we become aware of our bodies and most of us find it attractive when somebody moves their body with a certain grace. This is not to say we should all be Baryshnikovs, but there is never any harm in being more aware of how we move, it feels better when we move with the rhythm of the music.

Some say that you can see if people are good in bed by watching them dance. I'm not so sure that is correct. A while ago I met this young man who according to himself was an absolute spastic on the dance floor and I can only say that if the saying about sex/dance was true he would have danced like a cross-over between said Baryshnikov, Gene Kelly and Michael Jackson ☺.

In the same way that you can use music to de-stress, you can try to play music that gets your sexual urges going and feel how you would like to express the inspiration that occurs, either by yourself or with someone. It is fun to talk to people about what kind of music they find sexy and not. As with most things it differs from person to person and some people almost get aggressive when you tell them what you like. Now, the thing is that sex, just like music, not always gets triggered by the same emotional state, sometimes you want "wham bam thank you mam"-sex and sometimes you want the slow, intensely heartfelt sex and of course there would be different pieces of music that would work in those separate cases. But as I see it, there is sexy music and then there is unsexy music. I don't like to listen to unsexy music no matter how I feel. Sexy music is in my world just better and more enjoyable than unsexy music.

I know I might get half or more of Sweden's population against me when I say that Swedish so called dance music, which is a very bland form of country and western, is a perfect example of completely unsexy music, or almost asexual in my ears. It couldn't make me feel anything else than possibly a slight or huge irritation, like a drill at a low volume or something else that is neutral and monotonous. But there are other genres that I also find unsexy such as jazz, especially the kind which I can only describe as a bunch of musicians that seem to use their instruments in some kind of introverted masturbation, no melodies, no discernible rhythm. I also don't appreciate Swedish folk music, harmonicas and violins just don't do it for me, metal rock and other types of rock that sound more like a carpet of noise, (yes I am middle aged)....maybe it's better that I talk about the music I do like and that I do find suggestive.

Here follows a short selection of some of my current favourites when it comes to sexy music, with no special order of preference

Inner smile – Texas, It keeps you running – Dooby Brothers, The right thing – Simply Red, Bittersweet symphony – The Verve, Time – David Bowie, Aquarious – från Hair, All right now – Free, Govinda – Khula Shaker, My sweet prince – Placebo, Give me a reason

to love you – Portishead, For the love of money – The O'Jays, Son of a preacher man – Dusty Springfield, Walk on the wild side – Lou Reed, I don't wanna be – Gavin Degraw, Cocaine – JJ Cale, most of Michael Jackson's music, Barry White of course, and also most kinds of soul and funk and also some rock like Dan Reed Network and Nickelback and then lots and lots more…..

Was a little taken aback when I saw that most of the songs are by male artists, have never thought about that before, there are of course plenty of great female artists, maybe it has to do with me focusing on the sexy right now. Sexy music to me is about a good rhythm, sometimes it can be lyrics, part of a melody, or a base line, I'm not sure that I could say something generic that I find sexy, but I do know it when I hear it. There are a lot of great sites on the internet that focus on good sex music, one of the better ones with a huge number of songs to listen to is www.xmusic.fm , where you can also comment on all songs. A few samples from that site shows that sexy music can be just about anything and varies in as many ways as there are individuals on this planet. I find that very inspiring and freeing and it goes to show that I'm not the only one to think that sex is something you can be inspired to by just about anything. As long as it is good sex (which means sex where playfulness, desire, tenderness and joy are present) you can just go on and get inspired and discover new stuff all the time.

When I used "sexy music" on Google I got no less than 109 000 000 hits. I am overjoyed that so many use music and think about this beautiful phenomenon as inspiration. Music rocks! I'll let a lovely quote on music and its effects on us finish this chapter on music and sex.

"Music does bring people together. It allows us to experience the same emotions. People everywhere are the same in heart and spirit."

SEX AND CLOTHES

We had known each other since we were kids. We had played together, gone to school together and then as so often happens, we had drifted apart when work, a home of our own and all the rest had been on the agenda. He had always looked as if he belonged in a wild forest somewhere. He had worn his hair long, unruly and curly which made him look sort of like a troll. Nothing other than jeans and t-shirts were present in his closet as far as I could remember, not even a shirt for special occasions like graduations or parties. Not that I minded jeans, I wore them all the time as well, but I did have other outfits. We had been really good friends, we had studied together, tried our first cigarettes together and we had even taught each other how to kiss even though neither of us had ever viewed the other as anything but a friend We had agreed to do this to help each other to not be too awkward if and when it happened with someone we were in love with. We had been just as enthusiastic as two young scientists trying out different experiments. We had been up in my room, kissed with our lips closed and open, advised each other on how to move the tongues for it to feel most appealing and we had laughed and giggled quite a lot while doing it. Now we had a class reunion, ten years after graduation.

I had thought long and hard about what to wear that night just like the other women in my class I would guess; I wanted to look as good as possible. I tried on a few different outfits, one "Ally McBealish kind of suit, in dark grey with a white shirt, I felt comfortable and safe in that, it was clean and proper sort of…or should I choose the black cocktail dress, a tight crepe creation with halter neck that left my back naked…hmmm, maybe that would be somewhat of an overkill. No, I finally decided to wear my super expensive dark red silk shirt that was tight and really showed off my slim waist together with a pair of worn out jeans and the dark red pumps, that looked casual but stylish at the same time, I didn't want to look as if I had worked too hard at it.

Most people had arrived when I stepped out of the cab at the restaurant where the party was to be held. It felt fantastic to see all the faces from the past in this new version, some of them I didn't even recognize. I looked around to see if I could find Danny. I looked for his big mop of hair and a pair of jeans and a t-shirt but didn't see him anywhere. Maybe he hadn't arrived yet. When I walked into the bar I saw Jessica and Mia standing talking to a tall man who had his back towards me. His hair, which was longer than most, was tied into a ponytail with leather bands running criss-cross over it and I tried to guess who that might be. I went over to them and he turned around – it was Danny! He must have grown more than five inches since I last saw him, his face looked sort of the same though thinner and more manly and he had a ring in his ear that he hadn't had before. He had a black smoking jacket on with shiny lapels, it looked very expensive, the jeans he wore were light blue and had a few rips and tears but they fitted him perfectly and the off-white flimsy shirt he had on was unbuttoned so I could see that on the t-shirt he had beneath it was a Manhattan Silhouette with the text "Do it but do it in N.Y." .We stared at each other with amazement and when he smiled and said: Eve, wow, you look so grown up! It felt like the years just melted away. We hugged and couldn't stop staring at each other both with surprise, joy and a completely new sensation of shyness

During dinner we sat across from each other and I feasted my eyes on him Of course I could see "my Danny" when he sat there talking but the expensive jacket, the hair that was combed back and the ring in his ear made him look so sophisticated and I wondered if I really knew him at all. When the music started he winked at me and we went on to the dance floor. After a couple of dances he took off his jacket and rolled up the sleeves of his shirt. On one wrist he had two silver chains that were entwined with a leather braid; his skin was slightly tanned and glowed like silk. A few strands of hair had come loose and kept falling down on his left cheek. The mix of the jacket, the N.Y. t-shirt, the worn out jeans, the ring in his ear and the long hair which was almost feminine made me take a deep breath. All I could think of was to take off his shirt, touch his soft skin, feel his strong arms around me, release his hair from the ponytail and just "do it".

♥

That our clothes can trigger sexual responses is nothing new and there are quite a few things that are considered sexy. For women the most common is sexy lingerie, nylons, deep cuts and short skirts. When I Google "sexy clothes" it results in 14 400 000 hits and if I Google "sexy underwear" the result is 1 850 000 but when I search for "nylons" I get the somewhat surprising result of 18 700 000! "panties" gets med 21 million hits. Obviously lingerie and clothes that are sexy interest us. You usually say that a man is a legs, boob or ass-man, that is he prefers either of the above. Even if it really is the body parts that are the focus of attention there seem to be a large number of people who are even more interested in the clothing for these specific parts. For men I'm not sure what is generally considered sexy, suit? Jeans? Sexy underwear for men is not as overwhelmingly abundant on the net, there are some pornographic underwear, but sexy? I just Googled "sexy men's clothes" and got 24 500 hits, and when visiting a few of those pages I have to confess that sexy isn't really the word for them. Briefs in different fashions are in my eyes not very sexy generally, you can see heaps of muscular bodies but with a tight thong brief it looks more silly than sexy. I will address muscular bodies and body parts later on.

To me clothes are important, but most important is who is wearing them. A couple of sun bleached jeans on an attractive man is sexy, a flimsy shirt, preferably silk, or a shirt with the pirate look, that's also sexy, (thank you "Jack Sparrow") a silk robe can be sexy, a knitted sweater, a t-shirt, a tank top....hahaha on the right man anything can be sexy, well almost. There are however some clothes items that never works, such as bowties, clogs, folk costumes, knee long pants, shorts and the last year's horrific so called "Capri" pants, old-fashioned caps, slipovers, club blazers, short-sleeved plaid shirts where the sleeves sort of stand out from the body (you know which ones I mean), old y-front briefs that reach all the way up to and past the navel – PLEASE!

But back to what is sexy. I like a man who has the guts to be a little feminine, no I am not talking about men who wear dresses, but as an example I can mention Sting who at a Victoria Secrets show sang in a pair of black trousers that were so wide they could have been taken for a skirt, and I for one found that very sexy. A man who dares to stand out in that way signals confidence, which is always sexy. Jewellery on men can be very sexy too, not those thick golden pimp-chains worn with an unbuttoned shirt showing off a hairy chest, no, sophisticated jewellery that has class, like thin chains, earrings (yes it can be very sexy if you dare to use something besides a ring or a "diamond" stud), though I can't stand those new things where they stretch their ears to make holes large enough to poke your finger thru, they look icky, bracelets that have a cool design can also work. I don't include piercings in general since I usually find too many piercings to ruin peoples looks instead of the other way around. Generous shawls have become popular for men and I think that's great and to be preferred to those who wear a scarf thin as a tie tucked around their necks.

I for one, like men with a bit of a rock look, not the exaggerated biker boys, but rock is good, jeans, leather jacket, pierced ears, good looking boots. Good suits also work, but they have to be truly good quality suits. A jacket such as an Armani suit jacket together with jeans and a t-shirt is a classic as well and these examples are the most common when I ask around for what women prefer. Quality in shirts, t-shirts, jeans and suits is important even if I couldn't care any less about brands as such, but just as important is to be able to combine outfits to make them work. Handbags or bags in general almost never look good on men.

If I look around today, in Stockholm, there are so many men who don't seem to have a clue that there are quite a few women who like something else than bald, semi-overweight guys who don't seem to give a flying f-k about how they look. On the other hand the city is brimming with women who seem to spend several hours in front of their mirrors trying to look their best. Why is it that men no longer seem to care how they look, is it because they can land a beautiful woman any way? It feels kind of unfair and also unequal that women try so hard while the men don't put any effort into it at all. If you randomly picked a hundred women and a hundred men and put them next to each it would be obvious that women are more aware that their appearance plays a part on the impact on the opposite sex. Let's be honest, most of our apparel and what we choose to wear is aimed at attracting the opposite sex even if there are factors like wanting to look successful, make others of the same sex envious or just to put on some self-esteem.

Not too long ago people said that you'd find the most beautiful people in Sweden, but I can't agree when it comes to men. Yes, well, there are a few young guys who look ok, but most men above 30 look as if they've given up completely. That's no fun for us women, we also like to have something to feast our eyes on. Clothes can be fun and not just something to cover our bodies with. The right outfit can entice the eye and the interest just as much for a woman as for a man. I'm not pro vanity to the extreme, but I do think we could use the simple means that are there to attract and make ourselves attractive for the opposite (or if that's the case the same) sex. I've heard dozens of men complaining about how their women after a while into a relationship begin to wear sweatpants, wear their hair in an untidy bun and generally let themselves go, say: "Don't they understand that they're killing the attraction!" I'm just wondering, considering how men look today: "Don't you understand, you are completely killing the attraction and the sex appeal!" Joking aside, I think women should demand the same kind of willingness to please from men as they do from themselves. Earl Wilson was very close to saying this in one of the best ways possible: *"Women's liberation will not be achieved until a woman can become paunchy and bald and still think that she's attractive to the opposite sex."*

Though truth be told, us women have a lot more to choose from when it comes to dressing sexy. We have sexy lingerie, garter belts, which some people think are the ultimate sexy clothing, stockings, lace and silk. Some even claim that pantyhose are sexy, which surprised me since I have been brainwashed with the notion that pantyhose, together with sweatpants and old washed out bra's are the most asexual items we could wear. But if you have a look at the net, there is an enormous interest in pantyhose. I have of course always heard that women's legs are sexy, but that the actual material of nylon or pantyhose is sexy was news to me up until recently. In many sites it's noticeable that many men have a yearning back to the forties where women were usually wearing nylons with skirts and dresses. The classics in women's clothing are really making a come-back on those pages. What surprised me even further, despite the fact that I do admire a man who is comfortable with his feminine side, is that quite a few men seem to like to wear them themselves. A man with great legs who wears a garter belt and nylons and a twinkle in his eye, sort of like Dr Frankenfurter in The Rocky Horror Picture Show, I can live with, but a man in pantyhose, nope that doesn't spell sex to me. In the name of equality I must confess that I don't find females in pantyhose sexy either. Clothes that accentuate our best traits, whatever they may be, are actually doing the same thing as a beautiful and appetizing presented plate of food does to our appetite compared to a heap of edibles mixed in a pile would.

Clothes may be worn for a lot of reasons, but one that can be used is to sort of just let people get a glimpse or an idea of what is beneath instead of presenting the "naked truth" in one blow. See-thru negligees are an excellent and classic example even if that is also a bit on the obvious side. But a sheer shirt, unbuttoned just enough or a t-shirt on a woman where you can see the contours of her breasts can be more sexy than nakedness. It all has to do with putting our fantasies in motion. We know today that our brains are supposedly our most vital sexual organ, it's where it all starts, it's there our fantasies get a chance to develop and grow. Our fantasies or our creative minds are a force that can increase our sexual appetites better than most other things, if we use it wisely. That's why, it's so important that we do whatever we can to do just that, get the creative mind in motion, both within ourselves and of course within the minds of the opposite sex we aim to attract. Our clothes signal how we think and what we like, if a guy looks like a walking laundry basket, our minds won't take us to much else than laundry, but should a guy be wearing a regular t-shirt and a pair of jeans but also have for example a zebra patterned belt, we might start to think that there might be something wild in this guy or anyway that there's more to this guy than meets the eye.

♥

We're all aware that the balance between sexy and too much is vital. A woman having gigantic breasts who shows too much cleavage, or a skirt that's too short and doesn't leave anything to our imagination isn't sexy, there's no excitement there. Just as it's not sexy with men who wear those tiny thongs or a shirt that is unbuttoned all the way down to the navel exposing a hairy chest that we then have to look at whether we like to or not. The sexual appetite is better awakened with a bit of sophistication, not showing too much that is, but maybe wearing accessories or details that can intrigue and entice the eye. It's comparable to planning a great dinner, you wouldn't serve a heavy slice of meatloaf as an appetizer.

The limits for what is too much have, to put it mildly, changed. There was a time when the height of sexiness was that a woman wore a skirt or a dress that revealed her ankles. Nowadays ankles won't cut it to be called sexy, even if there are a number of men who find women's feet to be the most sexy body part. We see so much nudity and semi-nudity that our brains don't react as strongly as they used to which is why it's even more important today that we do not over stimulate ourselves so that our sex drives and sexual fantasies go numb. Fashion has transformed itself into pure pornographic outfits, young women walk around dressed as the pop stars on MTV and use shoes and accessories that look as if they've been taken directly from a Dominatrix's dungeon. Hopefully what we see now is what usually happens, the pendulum has gone to its most extreme in the direction of the obvious and or not so subtle and now it's time for it to swing back again. I have already seen signs that many of the new fashion sites that show off corsets and lingerie has taken on a different quality that look more chaste. Our clothes signal strong messages and it doesn't hurt to think both once and twice before we as zombies accept and put on what fashion trends tell us to. Us Swedes sometimes curse our "inbetweenness" but there is something to say for balance, or as my mother used to say: "Too much and too little can spoil anything."

SEX AND BODIES

She had been out to dine with a girl friend. They had talked for hours and now when she opened the front door she realized how late it was. The apartment was quiet, no TV blaring and the lights were turned off. She went thru the corridor to their bedroom and saw a faint light on. So he was awake after all. She went to the door and saw him sprawled over the bed, the covers in a knot with the bedside lamp still on. He had fallen asleep while reading most likely. He was completely naked and the light cast shadows over his entire body. She went into the bathroom and hurried to get ready for the night because she wanted to get back in there so she could look at him for a while longer. He lay there, as vulnerably naked as is only possible when you are fast asleep. She put on the red tank top she used instead of PJ's and combed out her hair that had been up in a bun during dinner. Quickly and silently she tiptoed into the bedroom. She looked at him, his face looking all peaceful, he had the most beautiful lips she had ever seen, full, with sharp contours and she could, in her mind's eye, see before her how he smiled so that the dimple on his left cheek showed. She let her eyes continue to roam over his body, his chest rising and sinking slowly with each breath. He had no chest hair, something which he had felt self conscious about in the beginning of their relationship. He had thought that she would have found it so much manlier with a hairy chest and it had taken some heavy persuasion on her part before he had accepted that she actually preferred a smooth chest. She couldn't help but touching his chest and trailed her finger down towards his tummy. He didn't move so she continued. God, she loved this body, every nook and cranny of it. She let her finger trail down to his hipbone and let her hand rest where the hip became the lower part of the stomach. His skin was so smooth; she leaned over and kissed his hip softly. It felt fantastic to have him spread out like this before her like a smorgasbord of man sort of. She didn't want to wake him up but it was hard not to give in to her desire to touch him. She let her eyes return to his face, she wanted to kiss him, but instead she used a finger and touched his cheek, she let her finger gently touch his lips, they were so beautiful and she couldn't help herself so she leaned over and kissed them as softly as she could. He let out a small sigh but continued to sleep. She felt her desire awaken, almost like a wild cougar, watching and waiting, as if it didn't know if it was going to come out into the open or stay in its layer. She let her eyes wonder over his body again, his chest, his tummy that was just as smooth as his chest, down towards his hips...she knew she was going to awaken him anyway despite her intention of letting him sleep. She leaned forward and started to kiss the area around his navel, she softy tasted every inch, she moved further downwards and kissed his hips, let her tongue explore the soft crevice between hipbone and stomach. Even if he was still asleep she could see how he began to get hard, she could almost see the blood pulsating and filling him, she watched fascinated how his body now prepared to make love and she used her tongue to urge it on. Slowly she let her tongue move up and down his length and made him all wet and shiny. With a moan he awakened, grabbed her by the shoulders and pulled her up so that he could kiss her. He rolled her over and lay on top of her, just pulled her panties aside and entered her with a force that took her breath away. They didn't say anything, they just looked into each other's eyes and let the wild beasts they both felt inside, have their way.

♥

Bodies, bodies, bodies, never have there been so much focus on our bodies as now. People have surgery on every possible body part and the problem I have with that is that it now seems as if we all want to look the same, or mostly women. The boobs are to be large, round, hard and filled with silicone or saline, noses should be small and straight like Barbie's, the tummies flat, the butts firm and small, even our genitals are supposed to look exactly the same. The ideal for female genitals today is that they should resemble a little girl's. That's strange to say the least. Young girls start to dream about cosmetic surgery before they're fully grown and I can only assume that God in his heaven is shaking his head in some kind of bewilderment over man's stupidity. I saw a program on TV just recently that was called "The perfect pussy". A young woman of 19 put herself through surgery in order to make her pussy look like a five-year-olds genitals instead of a grown woman's. She was so scared she cried and the pain after the surgery seemed to overwhelm her. I have to admit it made me cry as well. But she obviously thought it was more scary to have genitals that showed that she was sexually mature than to have the surgery.

If that isn't the limit, what is? In this program a male, who by the way, had looks only a very devoted mother could love, (he was chubby, pale, shaved head as round as a globe, thin slits for eyes and lips just as thin, a floppy stomach that hung over his trousers and fish shoulders) was asked what his view was on the female genitalia. His response was that it had to look like a sausage bun, without the sausage, otherwise he couldn't be bothered with it! That he himself couldn't turn on a seriously sex deprived female with his looks and his attitude never occurred to him. It was almost comical to see this unattractive man puff up as if to say that he could have his pick. At the same time I could almost feel envious that this man who seemingly had absolutely zip, nada, zero to offer as far as attractiveness or endearing personality are concerned felt the right to both radiate and communicate that he was entitled to reject a woman just because he thought she had an ugly pussy. I am sure there might be women out there who might say they would reject a man because of an ugly

Wiener, but I doubt they would look as righteous doing it. Unless it was one of those prime "bimbos" who answered, since normal women seem so extremely aware of their own bodies' real or perceived flaws I'm sure they would at the very least hesitate.

There is nothing wrong with keeping your body fit and healthy. But it has to be with some kind of balance and common sense. A body that's been overly exercised and is fully packed with hormones is no longer beautiful; it looks like a human version of the "Belgian Blue". Muscles and strength are things that signal masculinity since the beginning of time, but a full-blown broiler is usually not even strong, just stocky and immobile. No, thank God for the Tarzan model, a man who is strong and fit and flexible. Health is always attractive and to try and keep strong and healthy becomes a signal that this person has healthy values in that area. Men who refuse to exercise altogether, i e the opposite of the broiler aren't sexy either. A limp body, with a paunch and a posture like a rotten Chiquita doesn't radiate sex, it rather radiates a man who doesn't even like himself enough to care for his own body. There are too many men who allow themselves to be, what Earl Wilson, so neatly described it; "paunchy" and more often than not it's also these men that criticize women's looks the hardest.

In the same way as when it comes to clothes, us women put in the most effort, we develop anorexia, bulimia and exercise like maniacs to achieve the perfect bodies and it's a mystery why men don't worry about it on the same level. Yes, I am aware that there are men who are just as worried and also develop anorexia and bulimia and who have surgery, but relatively speaking, women leads by far. It's not as if I want to promote worrying, but it would be nice to see more men with the self awareness and imagination it takes to understand and even enjoy making an effort to please the eye.

For a body to be sexy in my Universe, it should be inhabited by a sound soul and a warm heart. And even if I don't appreciate a limp paunch, thin arms with no visible muscles, a sunken chest or fat thighs, a body that's appetizing can be sexy without fitting the measurements of the Barbie & Ken world. By appetizing I mean a body that looks tasty enough to put in my mouth ☺. It should be clean, smell nicely, and be cared for in a good way. I don't see any reason why men couldn't or shouldn't wear skin lotion to make their skin softer, use a great shampoo and conditioner to make their hair look their best (for those few and far between men who don't shave it all off) perfume to smell nice or care for their hands and nails so that they don't look as if they've just been out digging with them (especially if he plans to caress his woman's body). I am aesthetically quite normal I would say and think it's a turn off with un-brushed teeth, unpicked nails, unwashed bodies, greasy hair, unkempt feet... And even if I wouldn't say I'm a perfectionist, clean, I like.

Sure I also have my ideals of how a man should look, long hair, smooth skin, beautiful eyes of any colour, generous lips, shoulders that I can lean on, nice arms, you know the ones drummers usually have, slender waist, narrow hips, long legs without too much hair and soft feet. Did I forget something? Hahahaha, of course, his Willy, the most important thing in the whole world, according to men anyway. Ok, it's important in mine too, I like a normal sized Willy, lengthwise, girth wise, preferably slightly larger than average than smaller, but truth be told, I think most guys actually have a normal size – that's why they're called "normal". I saw a program on TV where a bunch of guys in their late teens were asked how large they thought a "normal" dick was, and almost all of them came up with measurements that would have made it to the Guinness's Book of Records. The relief in their faces when they realized that they themselves had "normal" sized genitals was huge and you'd think that at this day and age guys should know what's normal and not. In this particular investigation many of the guys thought that "normal" was the same as those "monster dicks" they'd seen in porn. Correct me if I'm wrong, but when large numbers of the population think that porn is a good representation on "normal" it seems we haven't come much closer to "enlightenment" or even "civilisation", rather that we've taken a huge step back into the dark ages. When it comes to women I think the same thing goes, a beautiful body is a healthy body first and

51

foremost. Breasts can come in many sizes and yes we all want them to be firm, but if they're large or small can't be that important for the sexiness level of them. Just as I prefer slim men I think a woman who has not got an excessive overweight is sexier than a woman who has, mostly because I think it looks healthier with a fit body than an overweight one.

Sexy body parts can be just about anything. I find a sensual mouth that looks kissable to be amazingly sexy but also hands that communicates sensitivity, a muscular forearm where you can see the veins, small tight buttocks, the area where the hipbone meets the lower part of the tummy, a neck with a beautiful hairline, a lock of hair that curls over a shoulder....but as said before, if there's a sound soul and a warm heart the body sort of becomes sexy anyway even if you might have certain aspects that you prefer.

It leads us astray when we stare too much on separate body parts as if those were the sole road to happiness. The hysteria regarding different body images and ideals that we have seen the last few years has brought us further away from quality of life and quality in our relationships than ever before. With the assistance of media we have now seen so many female and male bodies that are supposedly "perfect" that we hardly notice them anymore. When "perfect" has become the norm the excesses start to kick in. It's no longer enough for a woman to have breasts the size of basket balls; they have to be so extreme that she almost needs someone to carry them for her. On TV you can see documentaries that show women that compete for the largest breasts in the world. Why? And what counts as "the achievement"? The willingness to go under the knife? The willingness to ruin your back? It's become a freak show and nothing else. We are fascinated by the extreme, but do we want it in our lives? There are quite a few who have begun to react with a counter movement towards the extreme and unhealthy body images, we don't want to see skeletons on the runways, we don't find cocaine chic cool, we don't appreciate men who eat testosterone like TIC-TACS, everybody don't want to shave or wax off their pubic hair, see women with abs like Tarzan etc etc. When our bodies are primarily used to show off extreme features health and well being will always suffer. Even if there are many who claim that they think that super fat people are the sexiest you have to ask why you want to live with someone who is in such a hurry to the grave and no longer can get around on their own. Is that love? Not much. Is it sexual desire? Not in my book, but we'll talk more about the outsiders later on.

Our bodies are miracles in everything they can do and everything they can help us experience. Sex is one way of enjoying them and the less we focus on how we look and how our sexual activities look, the more can we focus on how it feels. A relaxed body containing a relaxed and easy going person will more easily have orgasmic experiences than a tense body with scared and worried person inside. That might seem obvious and still we spend enormous amounts of energy on worrying about if we are perceived sexy or not. Better then to put all that energy into focusing on the pleasure, learn what works, be open to a new person and dare to experience everything as if it was the first time over and over again. With the right attitude the entire body, and I mean the entire body, is one large erogenous zone.

"I am convinced that life in a physical body is meant to be an ecstatic experience." Shakti Gawain

SEX AND ATTRACTION

He had always been very particular about how his women should look. Preferably brunettes, but other colours could pass as long as their hair was really long and straight. They had to look classy with expensive and tailored clothes. A corporate suit with high quality stockings and high heels together with a crisp shirt usually worked well to capture his eyes. He was attracted to women he perceived as successful, self-assured almost stand-offish. They had to be tall and fit; he couldn't stand a woman who was overweight, they must have small tight buttocks, flat stomachs and small breasts. They should have very little makeup, no red lips, coloured eye-shadows or rouge, rather a pale look with just a hint of mascara to emphasize the eyes. He liked women with a sharp wit, he didn't mind if they were somewhat arrogant and they absolutely needed to have self-control. When he saw a woman like that he liked to fantasize about how she would act in bed. He imagined their underwear, most likely plain white without any frills and laces. He liked to think of the women as cool, controlled and anticipating, not passionate or excited, they had to smell clean and nice, be as free from bodily hair as possible, have well groomed feet and hands, soft impeccable skin and most importantly they had to be quiet during sex. On one occasion he had spent the night with a woman who on the surface seemed to fit the bill perfectly, but when she got her clothes off she had started speaking in a foul language and moaned and panted so much he had been unable to go thru with it. He felt chills just thinking about it. He had tried to understand what *it was in all this that so triggered his desire but he hadn't come up with a satisfactory answer. Maybe he was just a perfectionist, he was very neat himself, all the way down to the tips of his toes and he would rather be caught dead than coming home after a night out and go directly to bed with someone without them both having showered thoroughly first.*

This was why he found it so bewildering that he stood there and talked engagingly to the woman who had sat next to him at dinner at his best friend's. She was everything he wasn't attracted to. Her hair was bleached in stripes and it was no longer possible to see what her original colour was. In addition her hair was curly and unruly and she tried to pull her fingers thru it to get it to stay away from her face but it just kept falling into her eyes as if it had a life of its own. She wore a pair of worn baggy jeans and a tight top without a bra (!) and on top of that she had a leather jacket she must have bought second hand. She was at least a head shorter than him, and her breasts were as large as her head, she talked non-stop, laughed at her own jokes and touched him every two seconds. It was inexplicable but she completely and utterly fascinated him, first he thought it was because she was the antithesis of everything he did like, but the longer he stood there, the more he felt, albeit unwillingly, that he liked her presence. She talked about everything under the sun and he didn't hear half of it, he just couldn't pry his eyes from her full red lips and quick smile that came and went like a snow storm in April. Without warning she fell silent, her lips didn't move and he was brought back to reality with a shock. He looked at her red lips one last time as if to make them move again, but when they didn't he looked up into her eyes instead. She had a serious expression in her eyes and when he lost himself in them it felt as if he had been drawn into the Bermuda Triangle. They stood like that, completely still and quiet, it could have been a tenth of a second or four hours. Without being able to stop himself he used his hand to lift her chin, moved towards her and kissed her on the mouth like a wanderer in the desert who sees water for the first time in weeks. Unwillingly they pulled apart, both completely taken by surprise, their breathing hard and fast. Neither one of them bothered to say goodbye to the

other guests, they almost ran into the hallway, put on their coats and hurried downstairs out
into the street to get a cab in a feverish haste to be on their own.

♥

How wonderful and scary isn't it to fall prey for a strong attraction? When the very air feels charged, every movement is registered, time stands still and a short intake of breath is enough to crumble the resistance. I have always felt it to be magical, because there is an element of magic in the experience of being so completely focused on another person, it's as if nothing else matters, all you want to do is to be close to that person, or closer than close. Attraction is a potent force, some say that the attraction signals that there is a potential for love, or that there is a "soul mate factor" involved that we just by using our mental capacities can't really understand, yet others say it's just a matter of pheromones and sexual drive. Whatever the cause it is an experience that beats most when it relates to pleasure and focus. We become as homing missiles and forget both duties and everyday chores if we are "hit" by a strong attraction.

I remember this guy in my youth who I felt intensely attracted to, I experienced it as if I'd stepped into a magnetic field whenever he was close. All I could think of was how to make him feel the same way, see me, dream about me, touch me....and when the day finally came I was completely blown away for hours. Now looking at it in the rear view mirror, I can see that that attraction primarily was caused by me seeing him as the "ultimate man". He was extremely attractive in my eyes, he looked very much like David Bowie the only "idol" I have ever had, though with a more masculine body. You could see in his eyes that he was well aware of the effect he had on women and he never hesitated using it. In my fantasies he was "the love of my life", it was not only his looks, he was a great lover, he was wise, warm-hearted, wise, tender, perceptive, cool, talented and sophisticated, and we were meant to live "happily ever after". Our relationship lasted for a couple of years, and I'm not lying when I say that the force of the attraction made me completely refuse to see him as the person he was throughout the whole first year. When time had passed somewhat reality started to push through the haze of the attraction. I noticed that I didn't find him very intelligent; he drank too much and I found him to be so vain it was laughable. For every time that he had had too much to drink the attraction level sank, and for every stupid remark a bit more and finally I could feel that the spell was broken and I dumped him. That relationship awakened my curiosity as to how an attraction can lead you astray, as well as to how forceful and compelling it feels, how wonderfully intoxicating it is to just give into it and just in general made me fascinated by the phenomenon as such. I remember that it felt kind of disconcerting to sober up from that attraction and it took me several years to realise what factors had contributed to its strength and intensity. I did realise however that this was a force not to be taken lightly and which was not that easy to question and or ignore.

Attraction has always had a strong attraction for me ☺, I'm fascinated with the strong physical sensations, the power of the "I WANT" and "I DON'T GIVE A RAT'S ASS IF IT'S GOOD OR BAD" kind of feeling that goes with it, together with the feeling of being so utterly and vibrantly alive you almost feel immortal. A powerful attraction makes many do stuff they later regret and that in broad daylight seem crazy. But even if there might be dangers with attractions I want to focus on the pleasurable and lovely aspects of it

It can occur with a total stranger, but also in a relationship that for a longer while has been solely friendly. Most of us have experienced that moment when suddenly everything changes, this person that you've talked to so many times, maybe hugged and cuddled with or even slept next to, is someone completely new. A gesture, a look suddenly has a different meaning and your entire body responds with butterflies and excitement. To me attraction always brings along a totally new perspective of the person, I want to find out all about them. I want to explore and discover and almost step into this magical person so that I can get more of this fabulous feeling. There is something primitive about it, as if it's the reptilian brain who tells me that I want to be owned or to own this person and the intellect may come up with a few protests and comments but they come in second. The more you mature and better understand and recognize the attraction the more freedom you feel in choosing whether to give in to it or not. Some say that attraction is just a matter of "crotch love" and to some extent I agree, since a lot of the physical sensations are very sexually oriented; at the very least you want physical contact. You want to touch, kiss, lick and taste this attractive creature. But the attraction is not only about the groin even if that part of your body is assailed by many of the physical urges and impulses that fly around when you're at the mercy of a powerful attraction.

Many books and even older publications portray attraction and desire as the same thing. In religious publications it is seen as something almost evil and something you should avoid at all cost. But as I see it attraction and desire are not the same at all. The attraction feels more like a blow to the back of your head, it appears like lighting from a clear sky or in any case rather unexpected. As I understand it attraction happens because a person at some point, by a certain look, comment or action trigger something within us that has up to that moment been dormant or buried in the subconscious. Something with this person tells us that we have the possibility to still a need and irrelevant of the kind of need, it manifests as an attraction towards this person and we most commonly interpret it as an attraction and a desire to have sex with this person. In the very meaning of the word, lies the fact that we are attracted, we are drawn to someone, but I doubt that the whole truth lies in the fact that we want to have sex with them. I believe it is a message from our subconscious or our soul, that here is someone who can teach us something about ourselves or who will help us feel more whole. More about spirituality and sex later on. Desire is to me, more of a conscious yearning, we desire someone we already know, traits we find appealing or a human being that we like or love. Desire can feel just as compelling but has a more manageable energy than the attraction that sort of pops up like a rabbit in a magician's hat and makes us loose our cool. When we speak about attraction we often mention chemistry, which more often than not is something we use when we really don't have a clue as to what is happening, even if science now claims that it's mostly all about physiological chemicals and hormones and wants to think it has solved the mystery of attraction. But the truth is that had we been able to explain it all with chemicals and hormones we would be able to, in theory in any case, use those substances to make ourselves attracted to just about anybody. That would constitute a quick-fix for all those relationship experts out there. ☺

Sure, we can increase our understanding of what happens in our bodies when we feel attracted but I believe that no matter how much we research how our brains are stimulated when attraction kicks in, which hormones that are excreted, which chemicals or pheromones that make us light up like Christmas trees inside, there's always the fact that we are individuals, with different psyches and/or souls and that means that we can't explain nor produce attraction artificially since we can't know for certain what lies in each individual's subconscious. Of course there is some kind of general attraction, the one I mentioned earlier, i.e. the one that for example shows that most men find a female body attractive, but what I entail in attraction in this part is the one that shows up without no previous warning maybe even in connection with a person we have previously felt a dislike for or who in no way corresponds to the type of person we generally find ourselves attracted to. The kind of attraction which is so strong and compelling we lose our footing for a while.

One part that fascinates me with the attraction is exactly that, it awakens a desire so strong that both judgment and common sense are completely lost. But, if we are consciously looking at it we can see it as a guide or as a tool rather than just giving in to it. If we live in a committed relationship an attraction to someone outside this relationship can be devastating unless we control the impulse, but it can also tell us something important, as a whisper from the subconscious that there is something to be understood here. The more consciously we approach sexual desire and attraction the stronger the experiences. I understand if this comes out as if I want us to control our desires all the time which I don't, desire and lust are energies that should not be controlled too firmly but left out of control they can lead us to ruin. Ruin in this context does not entail any moral aspects of it, but I mean we should, as grown-ups, be the ones who consciously choose our actions and not feel helpless when an attraction comes our way. There's something pathetic about people who don't have any skills when it comes to impulse control. They fly like dry leaves in a storm from different needs and wants. As if they don't have any kind of will on their own allowing their bodies to be their masters and anything the body (or ego) might want needs to be satisfied, preferably immediately, without any consideration on whether it's sane or not.

Attraction is a strong power, an attraction can feel just as compelling as gravity and in the right context it's amazing and awe inspiring. Learn to handle it in a conscious manner so that you can enjoy it thoroughly whenever it shows up in your life.

"Was he attractive? She was too attracted to tell." Audrey Beth Stein

SEX AND FOOD

She stretched and yawned as the sunlight seeped in between the blinds. She turned around and looked at him, he had thrown off the covers and he lay spread out on his tummy with his arms around the pillow. She stepped out of the bed carefully so she wouldn't wake him up and went out thru the double doors that led on to the small terrace of their bungalow. The sharp sun light made her blink and rub her eyes to get used to it. The waves of the ocean gently rolling in were no more than twenty feet away. She removed her thin nightie and let it drop to the floor and went down to the waterfront. The water was almost as warm as the air and she kept on going until it reached her waist. It felt like being reborn every time she went into the clear salty water. Her spirits woke up and she took a few languid laps before she again stood up and felt the soft sand beneath the soles of her feet. She shook the water out of her hair and went up to the house again. She felt as if she was the first woman on the planet, so natural so amazingly primitive to walk completely naked to the water. Thank God they'd placed these bungalows in a way so that each guest could have a small piece of private beach. Outside the front door on the other side of the house the breakfast tray had been placed, it came with a pot of coffee, freshly baked bread and a large platter of exotic fruits. She looked at the fruit, mangoes in thin slices, strawberries, figs split in halves, melon….she took a fig and let her teeth sink into the soft sweet flesh. He stirred a little, stretched and turned to look at her with a sleepy smile.

– Good morning, already hungry?

– Mmmm I had a quick morning swim and I couldn't help starting without you. He stood up.

-Wait for me, I'll just go and get wet as well, don't eat all of it! He smiled at her and with a few quick steps he was in the water. This was as close to paradise as you could get she thought to herself when she sat there in bed waiting for him to return. Wet and shimmering he came into the room, and despite his small paunch and his unshaved chin, she thought he looked like some sort of a Greek god. He sat down in bed again.

–Aren't you even going to dry off first?

–Nope, I'm hungry, give me the tray.

They sat there and ate in silence for a while. She took a large bite of a melon and felt how the juices ran down her chin. He looked at her, put the tray on the floor beside her, kissed her and licked the juice from the melon from her chin and reached down to take a strawberry from the plate. He held the red berry in front of her mouth just out of reach, teasing her so that she only barely could bite into it, then he put it in his own mouth and kissed her so that they shared the strawberry which was crushed between their lips and tongues. She could feel the juices running down her neck and further down her breast and he let his fingers trail along after it. He reached for another fruit and came up with one of the halved figs. He looked intensely into her eyes as he held the fig up and licked its brownish red pulp. Even though he didn't touch her at that moment it felt as if it was her his tongue had explored. She almost felt hypnotized by the sight of his tongue against the fig's semi transparent surface. He bit off a small part of the fig and then let the rest of it trail her neck all the way down to her breasts where it left small traces of sweet juice and tiny brown pits. He fed her the remaining fig half to eat while he concentrated on cleaning up the pits and juice from her breasts. While softly tasting her he dipped one of his fingers in the now melting butter. He let his finger trail her hipbone, towards the inside of her thigh and she could feel how his slippery finger made her whole pelvic area shiver. For a short while he let his tongue leave her breasts to once again look her in the eyes while he simultaneously dipped his finger in the butter bowl one more time. He let his finger return to the soft inside of her thigh and let it teasingly circle the area until she gasped with desire. She found it hard to contain herself now and wanted more than anything that he should give her what she wanted but he quieted her breathing with yet another kiss. He slid down so that he lay with his face at her hips and she spread her legs so that she lay there completely open before him. He then reached for the bowl of butter and emptied the entire content over her pelvic bone and let it trickle down her hips. The butter melted even further when in contact with her warm skin and small trickles found their way down between her legs. With one hand he spread her open still further to let the running butter go all the way down. He put himself in a position so that he could get a better view of what he'd accomplished and let one of his fingers softly follow the trail of the butter. She felt his breath against her thighs and the excitement made her shiver when she felt his touch. Almost excruciatingly slowly he let two buttery fingers slide inside her and then just as slowly he pulled them back out. He repeated this while he studied the phenomena as if he couldn't tear his eyes away from it. When she felt she could take it any longer he moved his body so that it pressed against hers and slid all the way up to her making the remains of the butter, the fruit juices, the sea water and their own sweat mix between them. They kissed almost violently and he had her then and there with an intensity and abandon that almost made them stop breathing.

♥

Food has been used during all times as aphrodisiacs. If you Google "sexy food" you get approximately 200 million hits. Sexy food isn't just foods that are nice to eat in bed, such as whipped cream, chocolate mousse, different ice cream toppings such as caramel sauce, chocolate sauce and other things that easily can be licked off of the other person's body. Sexy food is also food that contains substances that can affect the sexual drive. Oysters would be the most commonly thought of when you speak about sexy foods. Whether an oyster is sexy or not is up for debate, a tiny slimy thingy that lives and is supposed to tighten up before you can eat it (and besides according to those who have tried it taste like sea water) – but, they top the list on several lists. That oysters are super expensive and luxurious most likely contributes to the position on top of these lists. But the fact is, oysters contain quite a few things that promote sex drive and health. Did you know that a raw oyster contains:

370 mg Omega 3 (vitally important fatty acid), 16 mg Omega 6, A-vitamin, B6 and C a substantial amount of B12, folic acid, riboflavin and B5. Oysters are also loaded with minerals such as calcium, iron, magnesium, potassium, phosphor, copper, manganese and selenium. In addition a single oyster contains 55% of your RDI of zinc which increases the sperm- and testosterone production. No wonder Casanova ate 50 raw oysters a day!

A complete health trip really. Other foods that aren't "just" sexy but also very good for you are for example almonds. In the old days it was said that the scent of almonds awakened the passion in females and Alexander Dumas had almond soup every evening before he met his mistress. Almonds contain heaps of vitamin E and magnesium.

The avocado is a fruit that has been deemed sexy both by its appearance as well as because of its content. Some think the fruit resembles testicles some that they look feminine and voluptuous. It's said that Spanish catholic priests found the fruit so obscene they prohibited it. Nowadays we know that the avocado is filled to the brim with good stuff, apart from the healthy fats it also contains folic acid, B6 and potassium. Other foods we can eat that increase our libido (and are healthy in so many other ways as well) are bananas (we are talking content here, not just shape), figs (that many find have a resemblance to the female genitals) basil(for its intoxicating scent – it was even used as a gift of love in the old days), asparagus (which contains folic acid that is said to stimulate the histamine production which is vital to reach orgasm for both sexes) eggs (not only chicken eggs, also fish eggs that you let pop on your tongue) and of course dark chocolate (which stimulates the production of serotonin – the feel good hormone). Health is of course very important for our libido and it's essential that we consume all the vitamins and minerals that we need. If you can eat them during sexy dinners in a loving atmosphere – so much the better.

"Food has replaced sex in my life, now I can't even get into my own pants"

But sex and food is not all about health, minerals and vitamins. It also has to do with stimulating our sexual desires through appearance, scent, taste and sensuality. Everything that is slightly "runny", has a sweet taste and feels good to touch can be used as sexy food. This is why fruits like for example mangoes, which are next to impossible to eat without having fruit juice all over the place and which have a beautiful scent are a really good example of sexy food. Strawberries are less messy and easy to feed each other, as are grapes. All sauces and beverages work fine as well. When you start to play with food together with sex please keep "play" as the main focus. To allow ourselves to be messy with food makes us regress in age a bit and it feels a bit naughty and fun. When we dare to play we usually relax more and the sex becomes more easy-going and less prestigious and mixed with laughter and giggles. The more relaxed we are the more we can allow our fantasies and creativity to run loose and try whatever comes to mind. Many have too rigid boundaries when it comes to "messy sex" but it's really not much fun if you can't relax. There is a value in returning to our childish sense of innocence and exploratory curiosity when we engage in sex, just as play is an important and valuable part in almost anything we do since it allows us to forget our shyness and also to be more present.

In the movie 9½ weeks, Mickey Rourke used an ice cube which he sensually and slowly slid over Kim Basinger's shivering body, in Sex and the City we see Samantha serve her hunk sushi from her naked body, there are no other limits than our own. Even fats of different types work well and have also been used as "lubricants" in sexual activities and work well to play with as well even if oils, butter, mayo and other stuff maybe isn't as tasty to lick off, they make our hands and bodies slippery and it feels different to hug, touch and make love. The thing about playing with food is that we get down to a more basic level. The food and play let us for a moment forget worries about whether we look good enough, are skinny enough, muscular enough, well made up enough or sophisticated enough to turn our partners on. The masks and the walls we put up around ourselves for protection disappear when we play. Sex and food also stimulate several senses at the same time, smell, taste and the sense of touching fruit pulp or juices that run down along our necks, fingers or whole bodies make the experience multi-sensual. We also allow ourselves to invite a sense of humour and laughter into our bedrooms (or wherever we are) and exactly that, to see sex as a whole, as something that can include both the awesome stuff such as love, beauty, warmth, desire and sensuality but also the smaller things like childish play, exploration, messiness, the ridiculous and the care-free create a new dimension to our love-making and we feel even closer than we ever thought possible.

SEX AND SPIRITUALITY

They had been married for over twenty years. The original passion had long since cooled off and even if it did reappear at times their sex life felt lifeless and frustrated. It was as if all feelings had shrunk to miniatures of what they once had been and none of them really knew what had happened. Not that they hadn't tried to spice things up but it hadn't worked more than sporadically. They knew they loved each other and wanted to stay together, but it was as if the fire refused to rekindle and all that happened was an occasional sparkle. Neither one of them was very good at communicating about their feelings and when conversations got emotional, it usually came out as accusations.

And now, they had just arrived at a Tantric Centre up north after a recommendation from one of her colleagues at work who in enthusiastic terms had told her about the "best weekend ever". They had made the reservation, maybe mostly to challenge each other a bit, to see if they dared or maybe because they both knew something new had to happen. Both felt rather nervous and tense when they, each dressed in a black silk kimono, went into the warm room where they were now to have their first session. In the room, the lighting was subdued and candles were lining the walls, they could feel the scent of essential oils and there were an abundance of large green plants that increased the feeling of slightly tropical humidity and heat. In the middle of the floor lay a square mattress covered with a beautiful fabric in purple and white. Their therapist, an American who introduced himself as Matthew,

69

welcomed them into the room. He also had a black kimono on with a pair of wide silk trousers underneath. He asked them to sit cross-legged opposite each other. He sat down some distance away from them so that he was sitting in the shadows. He became more of a presence than a person. They were asked to start by untying the kimono belt and leave it open so that they could see each other's naked bodies. He asked them to silently look into each other's eyes, to see beyond the physical eyes and see if they could see the presence behind them. Both of them first felt slightly shy and smiled reassuringly at each other, but Matthew kept guiding them further into the silence and presence in his low and calm voice. The silence stopped feeling awkward and slightly threatening, it felt comfortable, almost sacred. They looked into each other's eyes, deeper and more intensely than they had ever done. He felt as if he saw her for the first time, he felt the warmth in his heart, the warmth of how much he liked her, how deeply he actually loved her. To his own surprise he became so moved by the moment he felt tears come to his eyes, he left them there and experienced a sense of liberation when he saw how her eyes took on a different glimmer as she noticed them. He was overwhelmed by his love for her, he wanted to touch her, but Matthew asked them to continue without touching. She smiled at him and he could see that something came to life inside her, she looked young and vulnerable, it was as if the years just vanished and they were back in their teens again. They sat like that for a long while, without moving in any other way than letting their gazes rest into each other. Matthew now asked them to let their eyes wander slowly down over their partner's face, neck and body and then back again to their eyes. When they'd completed that a few times he asked them to remove their kimonos. They were now sitting completely naked across from each other in a cross-legged position which revealed their genitals quite openly to their exploring eyes. The next instruction was to shift between focusing on the other person's genitals and then back to the eyes again and keep doing that. They both could instantly feel how the atmosphere became thick between them, she let out a silent moan when she saw that he was hardening. They were still not allowed to touch each other. When he had reached a full erection Matthew instructed her to lie down on the mattress with slightly spread legs while he was to softly caress her breasts. He couldn't believe the excitement he felt just by watching her lying there naked before him. He let his hands caress her breasts softly and gently. He found it hard to keep the caresses gentle. When he grazed her nipples he had to breathe hard with controlled desire. She was also breathing heavily so that her breasts moved beneath his hands. Matthew now asked him to touch her breast more firmly and gently pinch the nipples. She shivered and saw that it took all his willpower not to throw himself at her. He heard Matthew's voice from far away ask him to spread her legs further apart and with one finger touch her from the navel down to her vulva and then slowly let the finger enter her and stay there. She was moister than he had ever felt her and he felt close to fainting with desire. This proved to be the end of their first session of Tantric sex and Matthew asked them to once again sit up across from each other in a cross legged position. When they now looked into each other's eyes they saw the strong desire and deep love in the other's eyes and both smiled as if they now shared a secret only they could fully understand.

♥

Can sex and spirituality really be a good combination? Absolutely! As I mentioned earlier there is for example Tantric sex practices that have a strong spiritual connection where sexual drive and desire are used to reach a higher spiritual awareness and to achieve an ability to channel these emotions in different ways through the body. Due to the physical potency in the sex drive and desire many perceive this to be the opposite of spirituality. But depending on the philosophy you adopt they can very easily function as two sides of the same coin. Spirituality is often linked to chastity and celibacy, but that is usually the kind of spirituality that is described in various religious teachings. Religion is not known for its encouragement of sexuality or the use of desire as a guide towards higher levels of spirituality either. The spirituality that is referred to here is the awareness that everything is energy and that our spiritual self can be reached by raising our energy vibration with different methods. There are a number of sects that promote excessive sexual activities, especially to engage in sexual activities with whomever has declared himself the "guru" for the sect, but those kinds of con artists are pretty easy to see thru. But the sexual drive and the exercise of sex where you are aware of and explore the energy and reactions are great instruments to increase the spiritual openness and awareness.

Many share the experience of having had sex that feels like Nirvana, as if yet another element has made itself present in the sexual act. Some say it is love and this might seem as mincing words, since of course it is a fact that love is vitally important and as I see it also the highest spiritual energy. But if we talk about spirituality without making the romantic love too big a part of that discussion there are ways to discover that spirit is present.

I have on occasion had dreams which have included a strong sense of lust and even orgasms that have had a different quality than the "usual" sexual dreams. Those have included a feeling that is present both within and outside the body. A magnificent strength in the orgasm that in addition has taken place without me or anyone else touching me at all has

72

made me understand that that kind of orgasm is in no way just a physical sensation. The fact that it is just as much, or maybe even more, a psychological or emotional sensation is nothing new, but the spiritual dimension raises the experience to a completely different level. It feels as what is usually described as being ONE with everything or sensing God. The feeling passes but is lingering in the sense that you know it is something out of the ordinary and that you wish to experience it again.

Without spirituality, love or at the very least emotional awareness something as fabulous as an orgasm can become diminished to something that doesn't give you more pleasure than a tiny sneeze, it's a waste of sexual drive and desire to not explore the possibilities to experience increasingly amazing and even more transformative orgasms. To get in touch with our spiritual selves we need to be silent and still which might feel impossible when we are consumed by desire. But stillness sharpens the senses and just as we can experience that our hearing is more acute in a dark room, stillness can sharpen the desire in a way that it feels like comparing a tidal wave to a small ripple on the surface. I know that many find their sex drive strong and powerful enough and feel hesitant and somewhat scared to strengthen it further. And, as I have mentioned earlier it is important that you are aware of what you are doing since a quest just for stronger physical sensations is a completely different journey than the spiritual one.

If you approach this in a healthy way there are both innocence and a certain playfulness present in spiritual sex. It's in the innocence, in the naïve exploration that allows and accepts whatever is happening, the greatest possibilities for pleasure lie. In order to have a positive experience of Tantric sex when trying it out, I would suggest doing it when you are already in a committed relationship where you feel safe and preferably go to a Tantric centre or take a class so you get familiar with the thinking behind it and understand the teachings. Tantric sex doesn't have to be spiritual but since it is based on our innermost beings it is there if you want to. Of course Tantric practices can both release emotional blockages and let emotional issues surface. It is not uncommon that either of the parties starts crying or expressing strong emotions in other ways. The gentle and quiet touching and the slowness with which everything takes place are, at least in beginner's Tantra, are features that enable us to become aware of emotions we didn't know were buried in our subconscious. Many exercises are also performed with constant eye-contact which also increases the possibilities to accomplish a deeper connection than we are used to. If you have issues with closeness but like sex Tantra or "Tantra-like" sex can open new doors that will give you a multi-dimensional experience and help you go past your fear of closeness. Closeness and openness are to sexual adventures like an amplifier to a stereo. To go past your own blockages and fears isn't always easy, but definitely worth the effort if you choose to try it. Many experience a huge liberating feeling in the simple activity of being naked with their partner, and I mean naked in the sense that we are not using any sexy lingerie to hide behind, nor the different masks and roles that we play to feel safer. To dare just be ourselves, without beautification of any kind is a special feeling in any circumstance. But to be able to be that naked takes a whole lot of inner work so that we know ourselves on a deeper level and also that the relationship we are in is a trusting and safe one.

So many of us have what might be called "mental debris" when it comes to sex or maybe primarily when it comes to our own sexuality. We live in a society that despite the so called sexual liberation and an increased openness still is stuck in a lot of ideas that sex is "dirty, disgusting, gross or revolting"....well you know what I mean. It's of course not that easy to say yes to one's own sexuality when you at the same time on some level feel that it is dirty or disgusting. We also have the opposite of that, people who so badly want to be seen as sexually liberated they take part in sexual activities which if they were honest and in touch with their inner selves, aren't really what they want, but have more to do with trying desperately to keep up the illusion of themselves as sexually bold and free. That usually doesn't last long since what happens is that they ignore their true feelings of desire and lust which more often than not diminishes the sexual drive and also creates a lack of integrity and self protection.

Spirituality on the other hand is in its very nature filled with lust since spirituality is in a sense the ability to be open. I'm not getting into any deeper spiritual discussions here. Instead I settle for stating that spirituality is about wholeness. All of us have experienced a feeling of wholeness at some point or another; it doesn't have to be in a sexual context. Spontaneously we can experience it when we do something we absolutely love, a sports freak can feel it when the home team scores and the entire gallery is filled with people sharing the same happy moment, or when an artist completely looses himself in his next brush stroke, or when we interact with animals or any time that you're completely focused and absorbed in what you are doing. Many active sportsmen speak about peak experiences when they exercise or compete, when they feel that they *are* their body and everything around them and they become oblivious to everything else for a short moment.

The last few years we have heard a lot about mindfulness, that is sort of the same thing, and actually something you can learn to practice. When you experience mindfulness, any activity, such as peeling and eating an orange, can be described as spiritual. What I am trying to say with this is that it's important that spiritual in this context shouldn't be confused with religious dogmas or ideas, rather be seen as a condition that every human being is capable of feeling and that occurs when we experience this kind of wholeness, so that what we do, think and are for a short while is the same thing.

A lot of this is about the ability to completely give yourself over to something or really get into something mind, body and soul. When we think about people who are dedicated or devout we usually think about priests or monks, people who in chastity have dedicated their lives to God or the church. But dedication and the willingness to give yourself over is what is

75

needed to experience the wholeness and transformative power that is present in sexual spirituality. Within each and every one of us lies the capacity to experience this. And even if there is also a lucky few who seem to spontaneously and without any conscious effort reach this blissful state, it is in fact awareness that represents the most fertile ground for experiencing wholeness or mindfulness and without exaggerating, that feeling is a small miracle all on its own.

The next time you are going to have sex, irrespective if it is with your partner or with a new acquaintance, try to do everything more slowly than you usually do it. A slow explorative and sensual kiss can truly be a small Nirvana, make a slow journey of discovery over the continent of their body, undress your partner slowly and gently, let your eyes feast on each and every part of their body, and even more slowly, excruciatingly so, allow your bodies to melt into each other the way nature (or God ☺) so brilliantly intended it, since that permits us, for short moments, to actually be as one. If this is your first encounter with spiritual sexuality you have a lot of wonderful experiences ahead – be happy and enjoy!

"There are two ways to live: you can live as if nothing is a miracle; you can live as if everything is a miracle." Albert Einstein

PORN

"Playboy isn't like the downscale, male bonding, beer-swilling phenomena that is being promoted now by (some men's magazines). My whole notion was the romantic connection between male and female." Hugh Hefner

You think porn is cool? Have you ever thought about what it is about it that you find cool? Is it the fact that despite it being almost everywhere, it is still somewhat forbidden? Do you feel shocked, enticed, disgusted, excited?

The clock on the nightstand showed ten past three. She turned and saw that he wasn't in bed. Had he gone to the bathroom? She waited a while – no, the house seemed quiet. She had perceived him to be absentminded lately. As if he was mulling over something or as if wasn't really "there". Their sex life had diminished into something that more felt like a "courageous attempt" once a month than anything else. It was very different from what it had been like in the beginning. They had been at it like Duracell bunnies. She smiled at the memory. It had been as if they just couldn't get enough of each other. He was the best lover she had ever had, gentle, sensual, loving….she had never been able to relax that much with anyone else nor enjoyed sex that much. But now, now they behaved like those old clichés of a tired couple who had lost the attraction and mostly "did it" because well, you were supposed to. She wasn't sure how and when it had changed, of course kids, mortgages and responsibilities had played their part, but they had kept their sense of playfulness and had at least made love three or four times a week. This last year something had happened. He almost seemed to avoid touching her when they were in bed and he looked very uncomfortable if she brought it up. First she had figured he was just tired and stressed out and that it would pass. But it seemed to get worse rather than better. Now she had noticed that he left the bed some nights. When she had asked about it he had just replied that he went up to sit and read in the living room for a while when he had trouble sleeping cause he didn't want to wake her up. She had sensed in the way he had said it that he didn't really want to talk about it, he just wanted her to leave it alone.

She looked at the clock again, twenty past three. She stepped out of bed and for some unknown reason she really made an effort to move soundlessly. The house seemed quiet and when she went out of the bedroom she could see a dim light from the living room at the end of the corridor. Slowly and very quietly she tip toed past the kid's rooms, looked into the kitchen which was all dark and further on to the living room doorway. When she reached the doorway she noticed that the light was flickering as if the TV was on, but there were no sound. Very silently she leaned forward to be able to look into the room. He was sitting on the couch with the computer in front of him. She saw him obliquely from behind. Nothing had prepared her for what she saw. From the way he was moving she realized that he was masturbating! On the screen in front of him she saw four men satisfying themselves on one woman. She drew in air and felt her pulse quickening. What the hell was he doing, was this how he "didn't want to wake her up and was reading in the living room"? She didn't know what to do. Disgusted and somewhat chocked she snuck silently back to the bedroom and lay down in bed. When he came back to bed she didn't say anything and didn't let on at all that she had been awake. He fell asleep in an instant.

The morning after she stayed home from work, said she had a migraine and went to bed after they had had breakfast together. She lay back and listened for the front door to close. When she heard him pull out the car from the garage she left the bed and went into the living room. For her it was child's play to check his computer to see what he was up to. She had been working with computers since the early 80's. Her heart beat loudly when she systematically went through some of his previous internet activities. When she saw the kind of sites he had been visiting she felt devastated. It was porn she hardly could believe existed. pages with sadism, photos and videos of women who were gangbanged by several men, pages with men being gangbanged by other men, men who were pissed on, men and women who fucked each other with giant dildos....she almost threw up right there in the middle of their living room floor. This was what he was masturbating to instead of having sex with her? She felt cheated, betrayed, abandoned.... She kept looking, pages with young girls, hairless and "innocent" that were portrayed in situations with men that must have been three times their age, older women with sagging breasts and sagging crotches that were being entertained by young boys, even pregnant women in group orgies. What kind of perv was she married to? How could he look at this kind of degenerate crap? In his computer she also found a folder named "customer info" that contained thousands of porn photos. There were all kinds of different porn represented in that folder. Some of the photos were so completely offensive and repulsive she stared at them as if hypnotized. She spent over three hours going thru all the stuff. It felt as if she was married to a complete stranger.

Whenever they had discussed porn, the porn industry, all those "poor" lonely men who didn't come any closer to sex than that, about the contempt and objectification of women, about how the availability of porn was detrimental for the young generation she had never in her wildest dreams thought it possible that he himself was consuming pornography to this extent. She wasn't naive, she would have accepted that he occasionally could check out some porn, but more in the "normal" way that men often do. Almost as if they still were teenage boys who felt excited and giggly from the arousal they felt. But this, porn of the most revolting kind – and the quantity of it! He must have spent numerous hours to be able to download that many photos. This was so disgusting, so perverted, so utterly icky, so sick. She turned the computer off and went in to the bathroom. She showered for a long time, it was as if she wanted to cleanse herself from all the pictures that now were stuck in her head and even though she scrubbed using really hot water and soap, and lots of it, she still felt defiled when she swept the towel around her.

♠

We live in a sexually liberated society and there are several advantages to that. For example it is something good that we have progressed in our development when it concerns homosexual relationships. If you by "sexually liberated" mean that you have a relaxed relationship to sex, don't have a lot of hang-ups and have the ability to enjoy it to its fullest potential I'm all for sexual liberation. But today a lot of the so called *liberated* entails that we are expected to be so extremely tolerant when faced with sexual deviations of any kind that it's no longer politically correct to be horrified, distance yourself or even say that we find something abhorrent. Many answers with the same mantra if you ask them what kind of opinions they have regarding sexuality that is outside what we usually call "normal": *"As long as you don't harm anyone else or do something against somebody's will most things are ok I guess."* And then they look pretty pleased with themselves for giving an answer they know will be approved.

Sexual liberation is not the same as saying everything is ok. Almost every one of us is born as sexual beings (unless we have some kind of injury in our brains or elsewhere that stops us). We have the sexual drive within, just like hunger, thirst and other automatic drives or instincts that exist for our survival and re-production. And as I have said in earlier chapters, I consider a healthy and active sex life to be one of the absolute best pleasures in life.

The sexual liberation has given pornography a strong hold at least in the western hemisphere. Nobody wants to be thought of as a prissy dry morality bitch. Debates are being had trying to determine the turnover of the porn industry and nobody really knows for sure what kind of numbers we are dealing with. Forbes wrote in an article on May 25th in 2001 that the sums that are mentioned as regards turnover in the porn industry are exaggerated, just as the porn industry often and intentionally exaggerate other things ☺. (When you Google the word "porn" you get approximately four hundred seventy million hits.) Other articles in the world press question the statement that porn is produced in expensively decorated high-end business buildings (even if there may be some of those) and claim that porn is primarily produced in small, unprofessional and shabby locations where things like health hazards, tax payments and job security or any other activity that would count as professional is nowhere to be seen. Today when webcams and video equipment are so easily available anyone can produce porn and that is exactly what is happening. But no matter how much money we are dealing with, the fact remains, porn is now present in most homes by the means of internet. Porn and sex is not the same thing. Porn unlike sex is completely devoid of love. Porn is often referred to as "anti-love". Porn isn't intended to stir any nobler feelings within us; it is just intended for sexual stimulation, preferably isolated to the sexual centre in our brains and/or our genitals so that we without thinking move from one stimulus to the other in the quest for new sensations and new "kicks". In the following chapters, where I write about porn, I might change my language somewhat to include all the usual words for genitals and sexual activities without trying to beautify them. Sometimes it's just so much easier to, as they say in the US, call a spade a spade ☺.

(I'm aware that it might seem as if I think porn only is about men using women. This is not so, I realize that just as in any other activity that generates money many want to have a go at it and of course there are quite a number of women who has stepped on board the porn train and are producing porn themselves. This means that I am mainly criticizing the cynical and cold attitudes that are prevalent in porn. But let's be honest, porn is steeped with traditional "old fashioned" and conservative "male" attitudes and this is not something that I intend to ignore or beautify either.)

THE "GOOD" OLD-FASHIONED PORN

No, I'm not referring to the kind of old-fashioned porn that portrayed women who posed modestly (I know everything is relative and even if it was considered as very risqué in its time it looks almost naive and innocent today) in old photographs that men, who normally never got to see more than the naked skin of a neck, hands or an ankle of the opposite sex, looked at and found very exciting. I am referring to the porn that is represented somewhat further along the time-line, which showed intercourse between a man and a woman, alternatively two men and a woman or two women and a man. By that time you thought of porn as something that only "dirty old men" and/or some semi-perverted pathetic men without a steady partner looked at. You thought of some unkempt old geezer who sat at home with a porn magazine or his projector and got excited all by himself. You didn't think of him as a sexual athlete or a stud, you thought ALONE, a wretched lonely man who wasn't able to connect with the opposite sex but had to make do with watching others having sex. I am sure it was a huge difference between how young men thought and how young women thought about it. Men (including society at large) have since the beginning of time had a completely different view on their own and other men's sexuality than that of women and I'm certain that there weren't nearly as many females who in groups sat and masturbated to porn magazines compared to males. But as a rule, porn at that time was not something that everybody consumed.

"Pornography exists for the lonesome, the ugly, the fearful - It's made for the losers".
Rita Mae Brown

In magazines like Fib Aktuellt and Lektyr (Swedish "gentlemen's magazines") you could at the very most see centrefolds of women who showed their breasts. But in the porn magazines you could see photos of people having sex openly without trying to cover any body parts or alternatively completely nude women and men in a variety of poses, mainly women, truth be told. Even if the sexual revolution was getting started things hadn't gotten very far. 1969, when the song "Je-taime moi non plus" with Serge Gainsbourg and Jane Birkin (the song was written by Serge Gainsbourg as early as 1967 and recorded with Serge's girlfriend at the time – Brigitte Bardot) came out it was banned in several countries for being too sexually explicit. That's almost hard to understand today when we don't see very many limitations to what you can sing about, publish or make movies about. What was not different in those days however was that porn primarily was directed and produced to satisfy the needs of men. It was male fantasies about women who spread their legs, who gave them blow-jobs, who were willingly fucked that you saw in the porn magazines and movies. Yes, admittedly there were some who tried to stay in the "erotica-zone", like the movie Emmanuelle, where sensuality was aimed for more than hard-core porn, hard-core as in unsophisticated footage of people fucking. As Michael Chabon so eloquently put it: "It is very difficult to fail at pornography". Throughout time it has been a classic joke that the story in porn movies is next to non-existent and that the acting performances come in as a close second. You don't need a lot of talent; all you need is genitals and the willingness to let someone take photos of it.

Porn in those day mostly portrayed "normal" sex, where people looked like people, I mean it weren't exactly the top actors who participated in porn movies. Most of the persons who did porn then both had flaws and body hair, features that have become almost exotic today. Since the majority of porn was produced for men by men porn has in many ways stopped or halted the development of women's liberation and the equality issues.

When I mention the sexual revolution I refer to the 60's and 70's "make love not babies"-movements. A lot of what we can see from old documentaries from for example Woodstock shows a young generation who didn't just liberate themselves sexually, they were abusing drugs most of the time in the process. That doesn't mean that the whole idea of the sexual revolution was flawed, but the drugs resulted in excesses and behaviours with unfortunate consequences. The idea of a society where love rules, where we are free to love (and make love to) whomever we want to as often as we want to originated from the thought that human beings can live in a state of love without fears, limitations, jealousy, emotional needs and in boundless family constellations. And, in our minds it might work, but we have to accept that either we are not evolved enough to handle it in real life or maybe that it's not even a desirable way to live. The lesson learned could be that any kind of love Utopia where drugs are involved together with uncontrolled sexual freedom didn't work and that without the drugs, the sexual revolution would have ended sooner. We as humans don't thrive without structures, we don't thrive by living without impulse control, we don't thrive by having sex with everybody we meet (if for no other reasons than the risks of infections and unwanted kids), most of us don't want to share our romantic partner with anyone else, even our very sexuality is damaged by too much freedom, it withers and dies...

The beginning of the sexual revolution was primarily an attempt at revolutionizing our views about sex, about allowing us to have more sex partners, and about seeing sex as something natural instead of something suspect and "un-holy". But despite the novelty of talking openly about sex and your sexual drive, the sexual revolution as well as the "good" old porn still primarily concerned sex between a man and a woman in the more traditional way.

PORN TODAY

Years have passed since the "good" old porn, that is the "normal" kind of porn that shows a man and a woman having sex, became just a fractional representation of the total output from the porn industry. And even if there have always been variations and deviations I think it's safe to say that porn today would have made our forefathers invoke the Gods or at least say that Sodom and Gomorrah now has risen from the ruins.

If you Google "porn" you don't have to add "hard-core". The very meaning of hard-core has become obsolete since everything is hard-core today. There are almost endless possibilities to watch free porn on the internet today. I can't even understand how those porn video stores still can survive in their cellar based, all windows blocked locations. Maybe there are a few people who still don't have access to the World Wide Web.

There is, for a lack of a better word, a gigantic smorgasbord of porn set on the internet containing all flavours or preferences you can imagine. You have to wonder about the origin of these varieties, but if we leave the cause for now, it is plain to see how these porn sites are designed to entice clueless people into more and more extreme porn consumption. I will get back to that subject in the chapter of how porn affects us and the society we live in.

The smorgasbord

It's an outrageously shattering experience to surf the internet for porn. We used to find it shocking to see same sex sex or group sex. But lesbian, gay or group sex are old news, and for some of you maybe everything I mention is old news but hopefully the majority will see this as unknown and untried facts and phenomena.

Some of the headings you'll find are: **teen porn, granny porn, redheads, blonds, Asian porn, Ebony, shaved pussies, hairy pussies, nylon sex, transvestites, transsexuals, bondage, dominatrix, diaper sex, wet sex** (people that urinate on each other) **caviar!!!**(poop sex) , **anal sex, stretching,** (trying to fit the most extremely oversized objects up their anuses or pussies) **fisting** (people who push fists up their anuses or pussies) , **animal sex, rough sex, whip sex, S & M** and a variety of different dominance / submissive sex) , **fetish-sex, pregnancy-sex, exhibitionists, dogging,** (people who fuck in public (with strangers) and/or just expose themselves), **amateur sex, big dicks, big tits, blow-jobs, camel toe** (women's genitals in too tight pants, panties or pantyhose), **cum-shots** (women and sometimes men who get lots of cum in their faces usually by a group of men), **double penetration, hand-jobs, masturbation, outdoors, orgies, porn stars, trampling** (men who want women to wear high heels and squash their dicks or at times small animals) **small tits, toys** and last but not least I'd like to mention that there is one (!) heading that reads **"female friendly"**.

This is of course not a complete representation of everything that is out there, and frankly I'm not sure if anyone really knows *everything* that exist in this genre, but this will suffice. I find it noticeable that there is only one heading directed towards women, not very surprising if we take an honest look at how society functions, but still, in this day and age.

Pain, sadism, masochism, submission and dominance

I find it extraordinary to find that so much of the porn really is more about violence than sex. S&M or sado-masochism, or sadism or masochism could be, if you look at it superficially, a couple (if one is into S and the other M) which represents a match made in heaven. But the porn that has this header can for example be a male who wears a scary looking mask over his head, leather bands strapped around his dick, a dog leash around his neck, leather gloves and maybe a whip. Usually these men are pale flabby and completely un-attractive and they are to force the woman into submission by manhandling her in different ways. The woman often looks kind of ill at ease (or maybe she's just a lousy actress trying to look as if she enjoys torture) and maybe that's the point, and the man is of course completely callous when she pleads or cries for mercy. This anonymous violent sex gives me a creepy feeling and I have to admit that I have to question how this can be associated with sexual feelings for anyone. In other sequences the woman is the one to dominate and torture. When this is the case she wears high heels, leather outfits, whips but not nearly as often any mask to cover her face. The man might be lying naked on a bench of some kind, tied down so he can't move and the woman struts around the bench dominating him by giving him a taste of the whip, a shoe in his mouth, or uses her long nails to scratch his skin. The common denominator in this kind of script seems to be that the "excited party" is in fact enjoying being treated in a disrespectful and offensive manner. Within the violent porn you also find bonding, that is, the victim is tied down and is defenceless, alternatively different body parts like the genitals or the woman's breasts have been tied in a way to make them turn blue, and for a person who's not into that it all primarily resembles torture.

"Pornography is about dominance. Erotica is about mutuality." Gloria Steinem

To be sexually aroused by watching other people being tortured or being inflicted by pain is to me not healthy. It has nothing to do with sex and/or sex and love. In these circumstances it doesn't even feel right to mention lust, what it is is some kind of excitement though I don't mean the pleasurable kind of excitement, rather a stress reaction that keeps the body fully alert with a twinge of fear. So when I use excitement here this is the condition I refer to. Sadism in our sex lives is just as abominable as seeing civilians being tortured by soldiers who do it to "pass the time" which recent updates from war infested countries have shown. Most of us react instinctively knowing instantly that it is wrong to hurt other living creatures who are defenceless, no matter what the context. I can already hear the protests from the S&M fan clubs. "But if someone wants you to hurt them, if they truly like it and even are gagging (no pun intended) for it?!?! "

You could figure that this is just complying with someone's needs and therefore something good, couldn't you? But I for one would recommend those who have this "need", whether it is to inflict pain or be hurt yourself, to go see a qualified therapist because I'm sure that something has become warped in their emotional system. Find out why you mix desire and lust with pain and learn new ways to handle it! I'm no expert when it comes to psychology in the sense that I am a therapist with a degree, but I have a truck load of common sense and I know for sure that there are no kids or other living beings who when in deep pain ask for more. We feel pain in order to warn our system that something dangerous is going on. A warning from the autonomous nerve system "knows" that something is happening that we need to be aware of and fix. What scares me the most in this is that when you watch sadistic porn you don't know if the receiving party really "likes it", or even have consented to the actions, it could be people who are threatened or coerced and really get hurt. In sadistic porn real pain is inflicted (try pulling a tight band around your dick or your breast until it turns blue and you'll see for yourself) and what you are watching is a person in pain. Is that really something you enjoy?

That violence fascinate us is obvious when you see all the "entertainment violence" on TV and on the movie screen. There is CSI, CIS, Cold Case and murder stories non-stop and all of them present stories about death, maiming and utterly disturbed murderers. The difference in this kind of productions is of course that no one is hurt since everything is make believe, there are camera men, make-up artists, directors, actors, props, set designers, you name it, who all cooperate to make us viewers believe it is all for real, **BUT ALL OF IT IS FAKE!** It is an illusion we are watching when we look at murder mysteries and personally I don't think it's healthy to watch too much of that either. The thing is we get de-sensitized or numb if we watch too much and when we see it in porn we don't react with the disgust and horror that would be appropriate. That is one of the reasons why it is important that you remind yourself and are aware of what you are watching in order for your natural instincts and reactions to remain intact and healthy.

When it comes to the milder version of S&M, that is dominance and submission, there is some other stuff going on. The way it looks from the outside this is more about having power or alternatively submitting one's power, but not necessarily by inflicting pain. There are grey areas in this of course, but I think it is adequate to separate these two when one so distinctly is about inflicting physical pain and the other has a pronounced psychological factor that is in focus. Anyway, there is a lot of porn which for example presents a dominatrix who in order to entice and enhance the "victim's" sexual arousal is showing her power by commanding different behaviours from the victim, like kissing her boots, licking her pussy, not move at all and submit to all and any of her desires. There is also the classical example which is seen more as the "female friendly" porn or erotica that shows a male who is such an expert and seduces the woman with such skill and elegance that she no longer is capable to resist or simply loses control. As long as this is done with love I could see it as a "play" with our gender specific roles and also see a few similarities with Tantric sex. The thought of submitting to someone who takes care of our needs is something that is present in so many

91

areas of life. Most of us have had our hair done, have had a massage; have seen a therapist or even something as simple as having our hunger appeased at a restaurant. In the sexual context it is somewhat more complicated to submit since most of us view our sexuality as something very personal which has to do with our over-all sense of integrity. Psychologically it's easy to understand though that people in this day and age have a need to be free of responsibilities and to be cared for from time to time, but it is vital that you give that responsibility over to the right individual.

Within Tantra there is for example something called Yoni massage (for the woman) and Lingam massage (for the man). When given a Tantric massage you give yourself over to the masseur/eus in a very safe environment which helps you relax completely and they use different techniques for breathing and relaxation prior to performing the actual massage of the genitals until orgasm is reached. The woman or the man does not have to perform in any way just lie there and receive the experience. The masseur/eus is in no way part of the sexual arousal and should be seen just as a hairdresser or any other kind of service giver, However, it does take a lot of understanding and wisdom as regards the human psyche as well as sexual liberation to be able to perform a yoni- or lingam massage. What I am aiming at here is that I can see the basic need of being cared for, or not having to perform, in the gentler form of dominance and submission with the difference that there are two people playing at this. You might think that this contradicts what I wrote earlier about the fact that sexual arousal not is a given just from physical touch, but this kind of massage is something you yourself have chosen and that you yourself prepare for mentally and emotionally, which makes it something more than just a physical thing.

Then we have the whipping thing..... Whips seem to have taken on some sort of "a trendy detail" kind of association. To use a whip or spank your partner, with the palm of your hand, a leather whip, small wooden things (you know the one's that look like the "girly" bat used in baseball in school for those who couldn't hit with the regular one) or some other kind of gadget has become something that seem to be sticking around both in normal movies and in life in general as many give each other a "friendly" slap on the behind today as a way of joking around. How this has come to be I don't know. As I see it those who like to spank somehow steps into the conservative and obsolete parental role that entailed putting the kid over your lap with their pants off and spank the bottom until either the kid screamed loudly enough or until the little behind got red enough to suggest proper punishment. Or, if we prefer to be on the receiving end, we step into the "naughty child"-scenario and allow someone to punish us.

In this the submission plays an important part. To lay down over someone else's lap and get spanked when you can't or at the very least are not expected to resist or defend yourself cannot be described as anything else but submission. Some say that during these types of punishments between parent and kid a sexual arousal could arise for both parent and child and that this is what has been programmed into people who like this kind of stimulus. I'm not so sure that you need to have had that kind of experience, but symbolically we have all seen the image of an angry father who spanks his child, or of a teacher who asks a young boy o take down his pants so that he can spank him with a ruler. The dynamics in this scenario is of course dominance and submission, power/powerlessness. The spanked person is in the above someone who is usually a virgin who is subjected to someone with power and authority who awakens the virgin sexually. Again there is an element of the forbidden, or taboo factor involved, such as the teacher and the student or parent and child, but if it is that or the fact that one person has the power and disciplinary authority and one who is powerless and "ignorant" I really don't know.

At the clubs and among friends it's now very "comme il faut" to jokingly spank each other's buttocks. The spanking is also very common in music videos on MTV and seems to have seeped into everyone's living room and/or bedroom. Songs with lyrics about being spanked or "spank me" don't surprise or shock anyone these days. It seems more as if it's become a trend factor and a standard behaviour. I can understand that people think leather outfits, whips and boots look pretty cool, especially when used by rock stars or other celebrities, but I cannot find anything cool or endearing in meeting a man who would in any shape or form try to spank me. The association for me would be that I'd met someone who finds spanking necessary to "get what he wants" and that the person in question has some issues regarding his own sexuality that makes him want to punish his sexual partner or maybe that this is a person who feels more powerful with a whip in his hand. If I had ever met a guy who would have even tried to slap me on the butt during sex I would surely have turned completely off , maybe wondered whether he was joking, but most surely I would have become very annoyed and also felt a slight concern over what this person really wanted – but hey, that's just me

Humiliation and degradation

Sadism, masochism and spanking of course all have an element of humiliation even if that's not always the main focus.

Humiliation seems to be really popular because the range of porn within this genre is extensive. Sometimes it's about men degrading men, or a group of transsexuals who forces a man to give them all blow-jobs while the rest take turns to fuck him from behind, or a so called gang-bang, where a whole group of men do it to a woman. It seems to be an important factor that the scene ends with all the men coming all over the victim's face. The purpose of this type of porn seems to be degradation, humiliation and defiling another human being to the limit. The humiliated person is treated as an object and not a living being, but it doesn't seem to be necessary to always use violence in everything that goes under degrading porn. Obviously there is also a huge interest to see people who choose to be degraded in various ways. Apart from the more obvious humiliation porn which shows a person or several persons (who not by choice) are treated as if they are devoid of feelings of any kind, (alternatively an attempt to make the viewer believe that the person gets really turned on by being treated this way – (usually not very successfully)) there is the kind that entail people who wants to be humiliated. This type of porn can be showing someone who is pissed on or worse pooped on.

I have to admit that I haven't really gotten into this kind of porn on a very thorough level, but from the stuff I have seen the thing with being pissed upon or just porn showing people who piss (again this is usually women, and even if men can piss on the women, they also have their semen to spurt so maybe it's something of an "overkill" to have men pee as well) very common. To pee on somebody usually also entails the presence of dominance and/or submission. Within the animal kingdom urine is used as a mark of turf and it doesn't seem too farfetched that we somewhere in the reptilian part of our brains view the act of peeing on somebody as an act showing that we dominate or own this person. I'm happy to say that it doesn't seem to be as common with poop porn. The very thought of it makes me sick. What makes it even more absurd is when you consider that most people can feel a bit nauseated just by changing a diaper on a small kid, and here we have someone who wants faeces in their faces, lick it or even eat it, and that's no kid's poop we're talking about either. Apart from the apparent health hazards involved in consuming someone's excrements it is for me completely impossible to understand how you can make poop and any kind of sexual arousal to be present on the same page.

When we're on the subject of poop I have to mention diaper sex, even if that really belongs under the title fetish sex. This is taking yet another step into the bizarre. It turns out that there quite a few men who feel a need to put baby outfits on together with diapers or in some cases just diapers. There was a TV-show not so long ago, a documentary from the UK about men with this type of turn-on. It showed us a regular apartment building in one of London's suburbs where "successful, accomplished, middle aged men" came to return to their toddler years for a few hours. The women who owned the establishment that serviced them treated these men as babies, there were cribs, clothes that had been especially designed to look babyish whilst in grown up sizes and of course also diapers and pacifiers. The men had to remove their male attire such as suits, ties, cufflinks and briefs to be dressed up in diapers and rompers with tiny teddy bear prints. Some of them wanted to be "breastfed", wet their diapers and some just wanted to be treated as babies in general. The women fed, scolded and talked to these "tiny gentlemen" as if they were about two years old. It sounds as if something Monte Python would have produced but it was real. The women told us that not all of the men wanted sexual services, but those who did liked to have their diapers changed after they had soiled them, some just wanted to be changed so they could be sponged and powdered (and jerked off) and yet other just wanted to sit in their crib with a pacifier in their mouth and rub themselves against a toy until orgasm.

To me, and I doubt that I'm alone in this, it looks ridiculous with men in diapers and I also find it a tad stupid to choose this way to regress to childhood rather than to examine those feelings and perceptions that have made them incapable to handle life as an adult. It was even more extreme since these men were described as pillars of society that out in the real world were directors, politicians or in other ways held prestigious and powerful offices who more often than not were also very wealthy, wealth that would have been put to better use had they tried to get help instead. Some of those men were married but felt they couldn't express this need to the wifey (and I think it was a smart move to refrain from coming home in diapers). That they all had problems with shouldering the responsibilities life put on them and needed to find a way to rest from the "grown-up world" doesn't take a PHD in psychology to understand, neither that most of them had what we might call "mother issues" to use psycho terminology, but the way they handled it was, to say the least, remarkable. It was

96

fascinating to see and listen to what the women who worked there had to say. They viewed these men (and men in general) as emotional retards. The jargon between the women was quite brutal but when the men were present they all acted like the proverbial "perfect mom".

So many people grow up with a lot of guilt around sex. Some despise themselves for their lust and sexual drive and this self contempt can generate a need to be punished. When this goes out of hand the need for being properly punished can make them turn to degrading acts in order to release the anxiety and stress that are a result from the guilt. If we feel guilty for our sexual drive and desire or any sexual feelings that may arise we will as an act of self-defence try to dampen our original sex drive. And then in order to experience the intensity a healthy sex drive generates the stimuli will have to be stronger than the guilt, and this goes on in an ever downward spiral.

If I should endeavour to find something human in this pee and poop variety of porn, I yet again want to emphasize that I find poop porn altogether disgusting and that is final. But if I really make an effort, I can understand that there might be a feeling of intimacy to let your partner be there with a hand when you pee, for a woman maybe to be the one holding the penis when he pees, sort of the same feeling as taking a shower together and letting your partner wash your genitals. To see someone pee (and I'm talking about something other than girls being out at clubs and using the restrooms together) and by that I mean actually watch a woman pee can be seen as getting a glimpse of something very intimate and personal and maybe the thrill is, again, that it feels a little forbidden. That would also explain why pee porn mostly is about women peeing since men tend to pee here and there in public and nobody sees that as watching something intimate. Another explanation could be that a woman peeing in some way is the female equivalent of the spurting of semen visually, but that's just a guess. It might be that it gives you as a woman a feeling of being completely accepted when someone you love can see you as attractive and sexy even when you sit on the toilet peeing, but to be sexually aroused and pee on somebody else, pee someone in the face or elsewhere is a far cry from that and seems more like an act of contempt than anything else. And....speaking about contempt.....

Gay, fag, queer

No, yet again I want to say that I find homosexuals, as I mean it, i.e. two people of the same sex who has fallen in love with each other, nothing strange, sick or weird and is to be respected as is any other love relationship. I also want to point out that when I use words like gay, fag or queer I use them just to describe a homosexual man since these are words that generally are used to describe just that. But the gay movement and their sexually explicit expressions has resulted in quite a lot of contempt, not only from the general public but just as much within the gay community. The Gay Wave that started rolling during the 70-ies may have begun to achieve the legal rights to fall in love with anyone even if it was the same sex, but turned into the right to have same sex and sex in every conceivable and unconceivable way inside and way outside of the ordinary.

Among other things so called "sauna clubs" made their entrance where men, usually in the dark, could get together naked in a room where it was allowed to touch other guys' dicks, give each other blow-jobs, get one for yourself or maybe fuck or be fucked. In the more extreme varieties of these clubs they could place a bathtub where one man would sit while the others could pee, poop or come all over them so that they after a while were sitting in a compilation of fluids and semi-fluids that most people would avoid getting anywhere near. This was not such a great idea considering the health hazards involved, in the dark it's not possible to see whether someone has herpes blisters, genital warts or anything else that signals VD's and men affected by our most common VD's including HIV/AIDS increased incredibly fast in the gay community. The thing is also that in the dark it's easier to be rough with someone since you don't have to look them in the eyes afterwards.....

I had a friend who was gay during the late 70's and beginning of the 80's (he died of AIDS later that decade) and even if I considered myself open-minded and in the know I remember one evening when he told me everything about what gay men did to and with each other. That was the first time I ever heard about stuff like fist-fucking, head-fucking, mice which they let into their anuses, fists with razorblades between each finger that was shoved up an anus, light bulbs, torches, electric shocks and a whole lot of other disgusting stuff. I am completely honest when I say that I found fist-fucking bad enough and I couldn't, and still can't get my mind around head-fucking even if I do have a vivid imagination. Yes, the saying goes that it really is a phenomenon within gay porn – to stuff someone's head up the ass of someone else! You'd think it was an impossibility, or I thought so, or at the very least a joke . I mean there have been a few one-liners served using just that. (One of my favourites is the one from the Friends' series where Ross is asked to "crawl up his own ass and die").

How anyone could think that it would be a pleasure to stuff one's head up someone's anus – for real – not symbolically – is too perverted for a mere mortal to understand. The same goes for letting tiny mice crawl into someone's stretched anus and when in there panicking and biting anything in sight just to die of suffocation, or letting someone with razorblades between each finger completely cut your ass to pieces or for that matter to put electrifying cords on your testicles and in your anus and then hit the "on"-button.....what, in the name of God could any of this have anything to do with sexual pleasure?!?!?!?!? When I had heard all this from someone who had seen a lot of it with his own eyes in his own quest for gay sexual adventures I was stunned to put it mildly. I'm sure there are even worse things going on in porn, but I think this will have to suffice to make my point. In any case, these are hopefully very extreme and marginal varieties of the gay porn.

But there is a cruelly in gay porn that seems to come from a deep contempt, not just for other human beings, but often for human beings with the same sexual preferences. It makes it somewhat twisted for the liberal gay movement when the contempt within the community is that pronounced since the jargon and activities in porn of course also will be seen and known by the general public. This was my first encounter with porn that went beyond any and all boundaries and it took me years to realize that this was true. For me it would have been a lot easier to believe that the moon is in fact made of cheese.

Why this type of unearthly activities made the impact they did within the gay community is debatable. One thought could be that it was to incredibly hard for homosexuals to accept their own orientation in a society that condemned it that they were filled with a bottomless self-contempt. Therefore, together with the blocked and repressed emotions of lust that also must have been present the contempt became an integral part of the sexual expression. No matter what reasons you could think of, this cruelty and crudeness that play such a big part in most porn today are horrifying.

You can also find porn where queers "seduce" straight men. It could be anything from high school boys to middle aged heterosexual men who up till then has been happily married who are to be seduced and convinced to get involved in gay sex. Again, you wonder if the "kick" is to seduce a "virgin" or if it is about the malicious joy over having succeeded in getting yet another man to wake up with feelings of guilt, anxiety and confusion when he has tried gay sex, especially if it's a man who has expressed contempt for gays.

If I haven't been clear on what I think about the crudeness and complete lack of all aspects of things like sensuality, connectedness, closeness, warmth, love and joy that this represents I want to tell you about the time, in the beginning of the 80's when I spent one evening at the famous disco Studio 54. As so many other disco ducks I was thrilled to see THE DISCO. Unfortunately it was gay night that evening. I noticed that the men, almost without exception had similar outfits. Hardly any glamorous drag-like queens – no, most of them were dressed in leather pants, a t-shirt or a tank-top and some kind of cap. It was different from the scene I was familiar with which was drag-show queens and a mildly decadent type of discos, because here, I later learned, you advertised what kind of preference you had by having a coloured hanky in the back pocket of your jeans. The colour or colours told the other fags that this person wanted to be fucked, pissed on or something else. It was basically a gay market place where the mingling consisted of looking for the right colour hanky and then nod a yes or a no thanks. No preliminaries, no small-talk, just a quick screening and a nod. Need I say that quite a few of my illusions about love as a prerequisite for sex got a beating that night?

Porn = freakshow?

Stretching is about getting the largest or most weird thing into your vagina or anus. It can also be about having fluids, such as milk, poured in and then when someone pokes a finger or his cock in, squirt it out. Pictures of this look more like some kind of Guinness Book of Records attempt from people who obviously are prepared to do just about anything to be in a photo shoot. I have heard stories from emergency rooms where people with this kind of affliction have come in to get help getting out what has been put in. It has been hammers, torch lights, wine bottles, dolls, over dimensionally huge vegetables such as eggplants, cucumbers and squash, or fruit like melons, grapefruits and avocadoes. The thought of having to go to a hospital to get a melon out of your anus is just too ridiculous and sounds more like a joke in bad taste than a story from real life.

People who work in the ER:s must become really cynical since it can't be easy to feel empathic towards someone who thought it was a great idea to stuff a wine bottle up their anus and who then can't get it out. What seems to be an unknown fact is that some of our internal muscles can cramp so hard that you can't get them to relax no matter how hard you try.

The first time I heard about people who showed off their ability to have anything else than fingers or genitals in their openings was when the first friends came home after a visit in Thailand. There they had witnessed the ping-pong trick; a woman who shoots ping-pong balls out of her vagina which was to be seen as some sort of entertainment and which apparently became one of the Thai tourist attractions.

It's not that easy to understand how this activity of stuffing objects up your crevices has become a porn attraction all on its own. In what part of the activity of trying to stretch an opening to the extreme by putting objects that have no business being there, lies the sexual excitement? Is it the suspense of not knowing if the opening is going to pop or not? Or could it be the freaky fascination of what is possible to stuff up there?

I don't understand it and just using my imagination to try to figure out what it feels like is enough to turn me off and feel certain that that is nothing to be recommended. Maybe it's easier to see my point if you've had a baby, I don't know.

Everything is relative and I must say that the porn heading *double penetration* at least has a more sexual undertone. Double penetration is when two guys fuck a woman at the same time penetrating her anus and her vagina, or alternatively two guys try to get into the vagina at the same time or that the woman shall have one dildo and one dick inside her at the same time, you understand the concept. It must be somewhat tricky for the two guys to get in there at the same time, often one has to lie underneath the woman and the other takes the more "missionary" position. If it's considered sexy because the vagina is crammed or because two guys are so close I'll let others decide, but I find it being related to the stretching porn either way.

Fetish & kinky

The words as such are used rather sloppily today, originally, kinky meant to describe sexual activities where you used *some* kind of gizmo that were supposed to create a greater intimacy between the parties while *fetish* or fetish sex was used to replace intimacy.

There are different definitions of fetishism or explanations as to what is included as fetishes. Many use the term fetish and fetishism the same they use the term attraction factor. But an attraction factor is something that you like, for example if you like brunettes, but it doesn't mean that you *can't* be turned on by a blonde, only that you find brunettes more attractive. An attraction factor is just that – it describes something you prefer, just as everybody has their own preferences but it doesn't limit or control you.

There are a number of fetishes, many associate it mostly to different materials like leather, rubber, latex and all these outfits that can be seen in bondage and S&M. But there's more to fetishes than dressing up in leather or latex. It's also about outfits and accessories that signal dominance or submission such as leashes, leather masks, leather straps, extremely high heeled boots, whips, tightly strung corsets... Apart from the most eye-catching varieties that look as if they want to suffocate the victim with the assistance of some sort of a rubber ball that they stuff into their mouths, (the term is actually *gag* in porn) most of the stuff above is what we have seen in the fashion magazines lately. In every shoe shop you can find shoes and boots that look as if they have been taken directly from any of these fetish sites and a lot of the underwear and party clothes we've seen in fashion would fit perfectly in these BDSM (bondage&discipline, sadism&masochism) contexts.

Nylon is one of the most common fetishes. Men who are nylon fetishist are obsessed by the material and often use it themselves underneath their regular clothes. They want to see their women in pantyhose and stay-ups; they masturbate in stockings and/or use the nylons on their hands so that they can touch themselves with the material. Some more extreme nylon fetishists pull the pantyhose over their heads and bodies and kiss and fuck without taking them off. That's something completely different than a man who enjoys seeing a pair of female legs in beautiful stockings which, let's face it, most men enjoy. No, as opposed to most men's delight when summer comes and many women wear skirts showing off their bare legs, a nylon fetishist finds a naked leg to be a complete turn-off. When I grew up, which I have mentioned before, pantyhose was considered one of the most efficient sex killers and if you wanted a man to be turned on you had to peel them off real quick. Things change (or maybe not, but I do know quite a few men who still want to ban pantyhose.)

Other fetishes, even if this list is in no way complete, are **panties** (men who use panties and get turned on just seeing them) **diapers** (which I've talked about earlier) **feet** (men who want to lick, suck and kiss a woman's feet), **piss** (men who need to pissed on) women who **smoke** (must have been a great disappointment with all the smoking bans for that lot) **torture paraphernalia** of all kinds, **stiletto heels, blood, rainwear, uniforms, physically handicapped, vomit** (to be vomited on or to vomit on someone else) **trees** (yepp, there are men who'd rather fuck a tree than a woman, they put their dicks into a hole in the tree and have some kind of intercourse with it − must admit that it gave me a whole different association to the word woodpecker), those who wants **incredibly fat people** to sit on them and of course those who have sex with **animals.**

"Erotica is using a feather, pornography is using the whole chicken." Isabel Allende

Bestiality − or sex with animals, is something that people often make jokes about. We make fun of farmers and suggest that they all fuck their sheep or cows. When I read Errol

Flynn's biography I got my first glimpse of the fact that some people have regular orgies with animals. In the book there is a story about one evening when one of these orgies took place. They had ordered in live ducks which they fucked and at the moment of orgasm they strangled the poor bird so that it's tiny body cramped in the death struggle. If it is true or not I guess only those who were there know, but nothing surprises me anymore, but then in the 70's when I read about it, I felt nauseated for days. To force oneself on a defenceless animal or any other living creature who is powerless, like small kids is something so sick it belongs in a medical journal and nowhere else.

Then there are other fetishes which are extremely unusual like being aroused by seeing someone trampling insects and small animals like rats, squirrels and the likes to death, or the desire to be buried alive, have sex with dead people, have a limb amputated, eat human flesh or wanting to have sex with mannequins or even cars, but hopefully those people realise that this is so disturbed that they hurry to get help from the medical profession.

The thing that sort of is the common denominator for fetishists (and the majority of porn in general) is the presence of BDSM, someone or something has to be dominating or dominated by someone or something else or someone has to be degraded or degrade someone or someone are to be submissive or force someone into submission, that, and of course the almost clinical absence of anything that even remotely resembles love.

Many think that fetishism is something that develops with us when we are children when we for the first time feel aroused or have a sexual feeling (without knowing what to do about it) and it is connected to an object or a process.

The desire becomes locked towards the object instead of what we usually associate with sex, the attraction and love between two people. For some I'm sure it's about the fear of being as vulnerable as you are when you love someone, an object is easily controlled. But that also means that a fetishist's sex life becomes controlled by the object/fetish and loses a lot of that which is inter-personal such as feelings of connectedness, closeness, love, warmth and togetherness. It's sort of self-evident that if you are more aroused by an object than by a person sex is something completely different than an act of love.

Recently I read in the newspapers about this guy who was a nylon fetishist, that is he couldn't perform with a woman if she didn't wear pantyhose or stay-ups. He himself wore stay-ups underneath his suit pants every day at work. When asked about relationships he answered that it usually was ok in the beginning of a relationship when the woman wanted to dress up for him, but that it always had the same outcome where the woman finally asked: "Is it me you want or my pantyhose?" He confessed that he was so stuck on his fetish that he'd given up any hope of ever having a long lasting relationship. That sex is not about love when we talk about fetishists therefore becomes rather obvious. I'm not saying however that someone with a fetish is incapable of love, but they separate sex and love and thereby limit their sexual experience to something that does not include the heart and the feeling of love.

Today, in the name of sexual liberation, it is kind of accepted to have a fetish, maybe because the word is used as a wider term for attraction factor. I don't think that many would like to say they have a fetish for something when you know what it really is – a limitation that stops you from having a wholesome and healthy sex and love life. I know that there are people who want us to think it's cool to have a fetish, but I can't find anything cool or hip with being so afraid of intimacy that you can't enjoy sex as an expression of love between two people that you rather have sex with dead objects.

Everything is not to be termed fetishes – large breasts, small breast, long legs, short legs, long hair, balds, body-builders, thin, chubby, old, young, hairy, shaved, we are all different and like different stuff, it is only when the stuff we like controls us that something has gone wrong.

There are different opinions on whether it is possible to free yourself of a fetish or not, but the fact is that many who start off with one fetish extend their likes to include more and more objects into their fetishist desires. And, no matter what opinion you have it is easy to see that we all change and develop in different ways on our journey thru life. For example, I hated olives when I was a kid; I almost threw up just by the smell of them. Now I love a Dry Martini with olives in it, I love olives as a snack or together with a cold beer; I can even get a craving for olives at times. It's all about what we prioritize and choose to change even if I absolutely understand that emotional blocks not are as easy to change as a matter of taste for foods. But apparently it is so that we sometimes choose the "victim-mentality" and resignedly shrug our shoulders and resign to whatever it is that limits us. It is still a choice however, and many choose to not change, to remain rigid. The question is whether it's not a matter of being so comfortable with our limitations knowing it takes effort to change that we come to a stand-still instead of continuing to grow. It doesn't necessarily have to be about trying to rid yourself of a fetish, rather to extend your repertoire so that it includes all the good stuff as well.

Transvestites and transsexuals, TSV, TS

When we say transvestite we usually talk about a man who is turned on by using women's clothing. Many believe that the man with this preference is a closet gay, but most transvestites are in fact heterosexual. Some research, (not sure how scientific this is though) show that over 10% of the men in the western hemisphere every day wear some feminine clothing underneath their regular clothes. Far from all of them go all the way and dress up as women, but it is more common than you'd think. Not all transvestites are turned on by women's clothing either, they dress in woman's clothing to feel connected to their feminine aspects on other levels. Movies like Rocky Horror Picture Show play with the boundaries by letting the main character, Dr Frankenfurter, "a transvestite from Transylvania" have sex with both men and women. In porn, transvestites and transsexuals have a huge following. There

107

are several sites specializing in men dressed up as women who have sex with women, but there are also quite a few where the transvestites have sex with other men which seem mildly related to the part of gay porn that finds it exciting to "deceive" a heterosexual man into having sex with another man. There has always been something titillating over those who transcend the genders and when it's been done in a clumsy and comical way by a man who puts on a skirt and talks with a high pitched voice it's often been used to produce laughter. And even if it's not politically correct to laugh at a transvestite the fact is that when we see a man with broad shoulders, coarse facial features (that no makeup in the world can conceal) hands as large as toilette lids stumble along in a pair of high heels size 11, it does look both sad and somewhat comical. On the internet there are several contact sites and porn sites where transvestites and/or cross dressers show their attempts to "switch gender" (with a varying degree of success)and invite others for sexual encounters.

As regards the transsexuals, those who feel that they have been born in a body of the wrong sex who have chosen to surgically change this as well as use hormones, there are opportunities to make money in porn. There is a lot of porn that show men (that is people who have been born in a man's body) who after surgery and hormone treatments have breasts but have kept their dicks present themselves as women (they use make-up, wear women's clothes and often wear their hair long) who have sex with other men. It's kind of confusing when what you first see is a beautiful woman, beautifully dressed with real breasts who it turns out also has male genitals.

I have only heard about one single example of the opposite, that is a person who was born in a woman's body who has kept her/his female genitals but used hormones and surgery to in all other aspects look like a man. She/he had not found it as easy to make money doing porn. So, this genre is no different, it is mainly the women (or those who look like women) who are in demand. The popularity of the transsexual porn may be an

108

expression of the fact that we all have both masculine and feminine aspects and when we see a photo of a live person who actually seems to be both we are fascinated. (But whatever way you look at this there is also an element of freak-show in it.) Still it's mostly about genitals and porn, sexual excitement by degradation or submission when the transsexuals seduce or violate other men. I guess many have heard the expression "she-males" and Thailand most likely tops the list when it comes to the largest number of she-males. I heard the expression the first time in the British sitcom Alan Partridge, where Alan secretively is very intrigued by she-males, or what he in the series refers to as "lady-boys".

Amateur porn

As with many other phenomena the pendulum swings between the excesses back and forth. During the porn industry's glory days (and by that I mean those days when porn really had its break-through as a form of "normal" entertainment) the women who made the biggest bucks were women with silicone filled breasts, flat tummies, completely shaved, well made up with beautiful hair. As if they wanted to say "Look at these beautiful women who are porn stars, look at these dreamy creatures, how glamorous they are, gorgeous and super attractive". PORN IS GLAMOROUS!!!! And the world bought the porn industry's make-over, to a point at least.

Anyway it was women who mostly resembled cartoon characters who "acted" in the successful porn flicks, they didn't sweat, they had no bodily hair, no love handles, they were acrobatic and fit to an extent it almost looked unnatural, their facial expressions looked almost as a travesty of excitement with their tongues sticking out between their inevitably red painted lips as a symbol for their horniness. The men were also well built and always had enormous dicks which never were to be seen in any other version than at attention. When the first enthusiasm had simmered down and the male viewers had had their fill of the" perfect woman" the excitement died somewhat and many found it all to be predictable and insipid.

Now when amateur porn is in, we want to see regular people – warts and all – who engage in sweaty, messy and not so handsome sex. Milfs (mothers I'd love to fuck) are more in than young girls; even so called Granny sex has a large group of fans. No it's no longer the beautiful, the well trimmed that are at the top of the charts, now it's ugly-sex. Ugly-sex is what we see when Jimmy-Bob and Anna-Belle from Niptandoo decide to tape themselves having sex. Maybe what makes the amateur porn popular is the fact that a larger percentage of the actors actually are aroused and after all this staged and mechanical porn, there is a "yearning" for porn that portrays some feelings. Why they tape themselves when they have sex could be because they think it's an easy buck to be made, or they are part of the seemingly never ending hoards of people who need to show themselves off for the public. Exhibitionists who want to have sex in public places or who want to expose themselves in different ways seem to pop up like mushrooms after rain. And I'm sure some of them find it exciting not to know whether they will be found out, but if you photograph or film yourself when engaged in sexual activities and upload it on the internet, you serve the public a helping of the most private and intimate parts of your life. Why is that exciting? Is it because your boss may see you, your neighbours, your kids?

The need to be seen is so extreme today that people seem to be prepared to do almost anything to get it met. All these reality shows that started with Big Brother clearly show that this is not secondary to needs and aspects like integrity, shyness, fidelity, dignity or credibility. To allow other people, any people, to look inside your bedroom or study your genitals in order to get the need of being seen met is to put it mildly, sad. It's also saddening that there are so many, both young and old who feel so deprived of being seen that they in desperation allow the whole world to look at their most private and sensitive sphere since that is the only thing they can think of that almost surely will get them some of the attention they so crave. The question remains whether this kind of activity can satisfy our deep psychological need to be seen and heard. Will we feel content when we hear that someone has seen our genitals, or that someone wants to fuck us, or that we have a great looking dick? Or for being so sexually liberated that we have sex that anyone is free to watch? Or are there other and deeper needs behind it all? (Yes, I am sarcastic.)

If you look at it soberly the fact is we all have genitals and the fact that we don't have the integrity to protect ourselves and our most sensitive parts I find somewhat disturbing and I'm sure it is not the most constructive way to achieve being seen. It baffles me how people can be influenced to change what we all have with us from childhood; the urge to protect our sex and sexuality and only share those with people we feel completely safe with. Today this instinct is destroyed all in the quest for affirmation from people we don't even know. Maybe it's time to think a bit about what kind of need it is that is met before we choose to let the world into our pants, because if you publish anything on the internet you never know who will download it and anything you have published is there forever – that's a very long time.

So, you could say that with the renaissance of amateur porn the circle has sort of come to a close. We are back where we started, with amateurs taping themselves when having sex, using some semi-professional lighting, presenting hairy bodies, overweight bodies and old bodies. We have now seen it all and hopefully it'll be difficult to think of anything new to do. Porn will never die but if you believe that the pendulum now has reached its highest point as regards excesses and freakish things, we might be moving towards a point in time where it swings back to a level where conditions and needs who belong in clinical psychiatry research remains there and stays out of porn.

PORN – THE DRUG OF THE 21st CENTURY

He couldn't sleep; it had been a while now when everything felt stressful. Too much pressure at work, his boss seemed to think that he could take care of five person's workload. At home everything just turned duller and duller, he was tired when he got home and she just whined about everything he didn't do at home. They had almost stopped having sex, he was too tired and he really wasn't up to it either. Every time he looked at her she looked at him with eyes that reproached him for not being "the man she married". He gently stepped out of bed. She was fast asleep and didn't notice him leaving. In the living room he glanced at the laptop he used when he had to work from home. He wasn't really sure what to do, he didn't want to turn the TV on, she might wake up. He turned on the computer instead and went on line. After a few moments of surfing an ad popped up for ladies underwear. He clicked on the ad without much interest and the next thing he knew the screen was filled with beautiful women in lingerie. Black lace bras, stockings, garters, see-thru panties …he scrolled further down the page where the outfits were more provocative. He felt a stirring of excitement. Wow, those were sexy women, long legs, large breasts…he clicked onwards on the ads that popped up on the screen. It didn't take long before he was at his first porn site. He listened to see if she was stirring in the bedroom, but she seemed to be sleeping. Sure he had surfed into one or two porn sites before, but usually in the company of one of his colleagues at work who wanted to show him something really perverted or disgusting that they all could laugh about

The entire screen now was blinking with different movie scenes where a dick went in and out of a cunt, large breasted women who touched themselves, small images of teenage girls who offered webcam sex, a woman who masturbated with a dildo...He felt himself getting hard and he wanted to see more. He clicked on one of the images and was shown a short sequence of a fucking couple, on and on, he wanted more and now he couldn't stop himself from wanking while he watched. The orgasm came so quickly he never had a chance to control it. Quickly he shut the computer off and went into the bathroom to clean himself off. Shit, what a turn-on, it had been a long time since he'd felt that horny. Now I should be able to sleep, he thought to himself with a happy grin.

The weeks went by and now it was more of a rule than an exception that he went up after she had fallen asleep so he could sit down a while in front of the computer. Sometimes he even felt annoyed with her if she stayed up too long One of the first nights he had sat there for a couple of hours and he had come four times in a row. He'd felt intoxicated and the rush just didn't go away it was a fantastic feeling. It almost made him hard just to see the laptop nowadays. Sometimes he could even be impatient to get home from work so that he could sit down by the computer and let himself disappear into the haze of horniness. He did feel a twinge of guilty conscience that he did this while she was sleeping, but it felt so good to give into it he really didn't care. Now he wasn't satisfied with regular porn anymore. From the start he'd gotten the rush from almost everything he watched, but now he wanted to see more, see other things than just normal sex. A couple of nights he had watched lesbian movies and images, women who went at each other with dildos, sometimes two, one in each hole, later *on he had stopped at bi-sexual porn and almost fainted of excitement when he'd watched two guys giving each other a blow-job. For a short while after he had come he'd wondered whether that could mean that he was gay? But he dismissed that thought and the night after he had moved on in the seemingly endless porn jungle.*

When a few months had passed with his nightly visits in porn wonderland he noticed that it wasn't as easy to feel the excitement. A few times he had tried to have sex with the missus, but his dick had refused to become erect no matter how he focused and tried to replay images from the screen in his head. She had asked him if there was something wrong but he had just told her he was tired and stressed out. The mind-blowing rush he'd had in the beginning was getting harder and harder to find and now when he saw a regular porn scene it felt like watching the news, no surprises no excitement. His quest for the rush took him to increasingly perverted sites with teenagers, really old women, gay porn with violence and transsexuals. One night when he'd been busy wanking to a sequence where two transvestites were raped by a group of guys he'd heard how she went up to go to the bathroom. He had prepared for this by having other web windows open that showed sport events. Quickly he'd shut the porn sites down and placed his robe so that she couldn't see that he had a hard-on. Just as she looked into the room with her sleepy face and asked him if he couldn't sleep, all she could see was him sitting there in his robe looking at sports pages.
– No, I'm just tossing and turning so I had to get out of bed for a while, did I wake you up?
– No, that's ok, I just needed to pee. Don't stay up too late.

She had gone to the bathroom and then gone back to bed. That night he didn't come. He didn't feel so great. Like a child who has done something naughty and she didn't have a clue. What the f-k was he doing anyway? He was married to a woman he loved, even if they had drifted apart slightly the last year he knew he still loved her. They hadn't had sex more than once since this all started. It felt as if they drifted further and further apart all the time. But

115

now when she had looked like that, sleepy and a little bit dazed and in addition had shown concern for him he felt the guilt growing and also how he missed being close to her. No, this would have to stop, all this porn, he felt lousy sitting there, almost caught with his hand around his dick. He didn't even dare to think about how she'd react if she'd known what he was up to. No, enough was enough! He turned the computer off and went to lie down next to her, put his arm around her and when she took his hand and almost still sleeping said; Night honey, he felt himself relax and fall asleep.

Three days passed without him trying to get into the paradise of porn. He had suffered badly from his guilty conscience and promised himself to quit completely. Then the fourth night she went to bed early. He looked at the laptop which just sat there on the table. Without thinking he turned it on and before he knew it the hunger for porn had him in a vice. The screen was yet again filled with promises of limitless excitement in the land where all that really existed was his hard cock.

"Pornography is rather like trying to experience a Beethoven symphony by having somebody tell you about it and perhaps hum a few bars." *Robertson Davies*

♠

I have touched on the topic of how porn affects us all nowadays; we can see the influences in a lot of areas, for example the fashion industry. If we had seen our teenagers run around in dominatrix outfits ten years ago I'm sure we would have reacted quite strongly. But today when we have seen MTV, adverts, commercials and musicals where the clothes and the symbols are used, our reactions have been dulled. How many female artists haven't shown themselves in everything from corsets to see-thru bathing suits, leather straps, high-heeled boots and shoes and alluded to sex both in dances and songs? We are so used to hearing about sex, see nakedness (primarily naked women) hear radio and TV-hosts talk about sex and read in the press about it, we hardly even notice it any more. We are

116

surrounded by sex and sex talk and soon if not already sex is a more common topic than the weather. In the January (2011) issue of one of Sweden's most popular teenage magazines the girl readers were encouraged to send in their best "masturbation tips" and in one of the sexual information shows on TV they also talked about advising each other on great orgasm and masturbation techniques. We are all expected to be easygoing and un-shy and find it fun to hear people talk masturbation techniques on prime time television. Porn's entrance into our living rooms has changed us and our reactions. No-one is shocked today if shown an image of genitals on TV. Well maybe a few, but not many.

Our expectations on sex and what sex entails is something our kids start talking about before they've celebrated their tenth birthday. "Fag, whore, dyke, fuck" are words coming out of children's mouths before they even understand the meaning of them. Young people have access to the internet and not nearly enough parents know enough to stop them from stuff they aren't mature enough to watch or even process. Sexual education in the shape of information on how a female and a male sexual organ look has become obsolete. That children have access to porn is more dangerous than many realize. It affects their brains and emotional development in ways that will show up later as problems and unnecessary suffering. That porn has changed our ways to have sex is nothing new. Today it's as easily available with sex toys as it is with buying a carton of milk. We are even expected to have sex toys like dildos, geisha-balls, whips and other stuff.

Thirteen year olds start worrying about not affording to have plastic surgery to enlarge their breasts to the size of melons; they quickly shave off any pubic hair and have sex too early in their development. It has become unattractive to look like a grown woman today. A woman is supposed to be free of bodily hair like a little girl to be viewed as "normal". Teens who fall in love don't discover sex organically any more. I have heard young girls ask each other if they have consented to anal sex as if that was a part of some kind of standard. No-one has told them that most porn actors go thru thorough enemas to flush their intestines clean before engaging in anal activities so that the guy wont withdraw his dick full of poop or alternatively poop will be squeezed out during sex. They don't tell you either that there is a risk that your anus will start to bleed if you're not very careful which severely increases the risks of catching a VD. To try activities like anal sex and suddenly find yourself in a poop-stained couch or bed when you have just fallen in love and before you have even started to find out all the wonders with being in love and having sex, is something that I wouldn't wish on any young girl or boy.

If young people are exposed to porn before their brains and bodies are fully developed it is just as damaging as being subjected to paedophilia. It's somewhat comforting that paedophilia is one of the things that are deemed ok to still be disgusted by and to condemn without risking making a fool of yourself with the people who use "politically correct" as a religion. We are aware that if a child is sexually abused it can and often will permanently damage him or her unless they are lucky enough to get help from a professional therapist. It is abuse to allow kids to have access to porn the way porn looks today. It becomes a shock to their entire emotional system and we haven't even begun to understand the effects of this yet.

Today many young boys believe that their sex life is supposed to look like a scene from a porn movie. Girls are expected to like everything from blow-jobs to group sex and preferably also look like miniature porn stars. The guys themselves live in the misunderstanding that a "normal dick" is huge and hard all the time – and that is really what the human race needs – yet another generation of men with performance anxiety due to ignorance! (There are many examples of young men popping Viagra in order to be able to "go all night" – not because the women want them to, but to have something to brag about). Porn also causes the equality debate as well as "women's liberation" to stop in its tracks and even go backwards to an almost Neanderthal state if we allow our youth to accept and assimilate the roles and phenomena that exist within the porn industry today.

Addiction to porn – a pandemic

But I'll return to the beginning of this chapter. Several sexual therapists and doctors have begun to talk about a new pandemic – porn addiction. Several million Americans have in different surveys confirmed that they have an addiction to internet porn and can't get out of it. Most of these persons also have problems with obsessive masturbation as well as the addiction to porn. Some have experienced such severe addiction they have problems with both marriages and work and some have even lost both spouses and jobs because they couldn't quit. There is not so much talk about porn addiction here in Sweden but there's no reason to think it would be any different here.

Today we are aware of the workings of the brain and we also are aware of the mechanics behind addictions of different kinds such as alcohol, drugs, food, shopping, gambling and anything else under the sun. As if those weren't enough we now have to add porn to the list. As any other addiction it affects our relationships, our spare time and our quality of life in different ways. The nasty thing about porn addiction is that very many of us work close by or with computers and also have computers and the possibility to be online at home. Internet porn is easily accessible and if we are not aware of the risks involved when on full speed ahead on the porn highway, it could end really badly.

Not that many know that doctors and researchers say that porn addiction is as strong and in many cases stronger than an addiction to cocaine. No wonder really, sex is one of our primary needs and when our brain has been exposed to these strong stimuli that excite the system so intensely it changes our neurological chemistry. Obsessive masturbation also changes the chemical balance in our brain and create such strong conditioning and chemical

119

addictions that very few are able to cope or get out of it on their own. In addition to the chemical addiction it's also so that when we experience something that we find very satisfying we, just like kids, want to experience it again and again and again... It is when we don't have our head screwed on correctly and just give in to that need to repeat the experience that the addiction starts. We are after the "high" the incredibly strong feeling we experienced the first time around. But when the high wears off we try something more potent. That is, if you initially got an enormous rush out of seeing a "normal" porn movie involving a male and a female having sex and you try to achieve the same level of rush by watching the same kind of sequences over and over again you'll notice that the effect diminishes. The brain gets desensitized to the stimuli since it is already familiar with the images and does therefore not produce the same sensations in your body. When we're dealing with porn there is also an element of fear involved, yet another basic and instinctive feeling. If it's fear for being caught watching, or fear because porn is seen as something of a taboo or the simple reason that we feel somewhat shocked when we see porn, the fear adds to the reactions in the brain.

In any case, the process is the same as for people who start with drugs of any kind; we escalate the stimulus hoping to achieve the same effect as we did the first time. You begin to watch porn that initially disgusted you and yet again you experience the strong sensations you were looking for. The fact that the feelings of lust are intertwined with guilt or disgust makes, strangely enough, the sensations stronger. And so it goes on, you chasing new highs, the brain desensitizing itself, you try something new and get desensitized and finally there's nothing else to do than maybe try doing the things in the real world until they stop working or until you do something really dangerous that entails you being hurt or being stopped some other way – or – you will have to face the fact that your emotional system has reached a break-down and is in acute need of repair.

The porn industry is well aware of how this works and this is why the porn sites are designed the way they are. On every page you'll always find something other than you searched for, if you for example search for lesbian porn you'll find an ad for gay porn, or sadism, or something else that still is "new" to you. This way the porn industry ensures that people get stuck and keep on surfing. It does seem evil, not when you have the sales figures and turnover in mind, but if you understand what happens to people who become addicted and the lives that the addiction to porn ruins. It's not that farfetched to compare it with the tobacco and alcohol commercials. Before we knew how dangerous and addictive these drugs can be the commercials also used images that suggested that if we just started smoking and drinking we too would be cool, successful and appreciated. We cluelessly adopted both cigarettes and alcohol in the subconscious hope that we'd become as sought after and handsome as the images seemed to promise. I'm sure many became addicted and felt tricked into it since they at the time didn't have a clue to the fact that both cigarettes and alcohol can be addictive and detrimental to your health. Now it would feel kind of in bad taste to produce cigarette commercials and I don't think there are many out there nowadays who are not aware that cigarettes are no good for you. That was a short deviation from the subject and it was more meant to state that information and knowledge is important, than a contribution to the debate on tobacco and alcohol. I am certain that we'd all react rather strongly on a commercial for heroine for example, since we all know how dangerous that is. Even though we are more aware today about the effects of commercials and the messages we are continually fed with by the media it is far from enough.

"It's just some porn, that's no big deal". Maybe not – it depends on how we deal with it. To be in a relationship with someone who is a porn addict isn't easy. I have read several stories by women who live with men who cannot quit watching porn. They feel rejected as well as responsible for their men being stuck in the porn web. They fear that they are not attractive enough, not sexy enough and they know that they will never agree to perform all the stuff they know their men are watching, but most of all they don't feel loved by the man they live with anymore since he prefers watching porn to having sex with them.

It is just like living with any kind of addict really, though this is so much more intimate since most of us view sex and sexual satisfaction as a part of love. The addiction itself is in command of the addicted person's normal reactions, they lie, they hide, they steal and cheat to continue to satisfy the demon. The addiction creates a distance in the relationship since most addicts try to hide the addiction from their family/work mates/lovers and even from themselves for as long as possible. It takes insight and acceptance by the addicted person to realize how his/her life has changed and how much time is spent in front of the computer (or away from the family/their job/their lover) and to become aware of the risk of losing it all. Most that are addicted to internet porn are somehow aware that they've encountered something that is stronger than themselves and usually they wrestle with feelings of guilt, shame and fear of being caught, but as long as they can they excuse the behaviour since it gives them some kind of reward that to them feels more important than anything else. When reading blogs and other articles about people who have come to the insight that they are in fact porn addicts, you realize that most have used their addiction as some kind of stress release. In order to get out of this dysfunctional method to handle stress they have to deal with their emotions, work on themselves and release the fear of closeness and vulnerability that also seem to be a common denominator in many "confessions". For some it feels close to a religious moment when they release all those blocked feelings and ask for help. If they have a partner who has the strength to stand by them in this process and who believes there is a chance that they can regain their trust, they are indeed lucky.

Intense consummation of porn also generates erectile problems for many many men. This of course is the effect of the escalation/desensitizing process. For a man who has used porn as the primary turn on it just won't be enough with a naked or even sexily dressed woman anymore to get turned on. Not only are the stimuli too weak, these men also damage their emotional build-up so that love, closeness, warmth, sensuality and safety no longer constitute stimuli that their brains associate with sex. Their sex drive has been isolated, become lonely and objectified and doesn't function as it used to.

Porn can very well be a contributor to the extreme increase in Viagra usage. It all turns into a perfect vicious circle that both generates a larger number of users for the porn industry as well as more people who can't function without medications. So, great news for the porn industry as well as for the pharmaceutical industry. And as we all know, it is sooo much easier to take a pill (quick fix) than to find out the real cause of the problem.

In one blog I read about a guy who wasn't more than 19 years old who had experienced severe erectile problems. He had been really unhappy since he had just met a girl that he'd fallen deeply in love with and he described his fear of not being able to make love to her the way he knew she wanted. He wrote about how he'd been on the internet surfing for porn and masturbating continuously for a period of approximately three months prior to this and how he'd been worried when he found it more and more difficult to get hard. He'd started to search for erectile problems on the net and had been so relieved when he found the forum for other men who had experienced the same thing and who had put two and two together. He had taken the advice in the forum, that is, he had quit cold turkey and refrained from porn for a couple of weeks and lo and behold, his Mr Jonson had come alive again and he had been able to make love to his new girlfriend without a hitch. His article ended with his conclusion to never get on that road again, that he'd had no idea that this could happen, how incredibly miserable he'd felt when unable to get an erection and how fantastic it was to yet again function normally so that he could feel the butterflies, the excitement and the force of the attraction that come with the infatuation.

When I read about the 19 year old I first felt sad but also happy that he had recovered. It is terrible if boys as young as that risk becoming impotent (not only physically but most of all emotionally) but also encouraging that our bodies and brains recover and reset if we give them what they need. It's clearly easier to recover the natural balance for a young person who hasn't been addicted for too long. But those who have been at it for a long time may need years to both re-balance the neurological chemistry which in turn entails, just as regarding any other addition, having to suffer through withdrawal symptoms as well as doing the work necessary for both mind and emotions.

In addition to the misery porn can create in relationships, in the lives of the addicts and in society in general we have all those who work in the porn industry. No matter how much they want to let on that it's "just another job", we all know that that's not really true. The porn industry has spent billions trying to convince us that everything we see in porn flicks is voluntary and has been made with super horny persons who like it, and they have succeeded surprisingly well. But, take a minute, and reflect on what it would be like to have your wife come home after a day's work with sperm from strangers in every crevice, or to have your son spend his work day by having two she-males fuck his ass and mouth, or your daughter telling you about the gang-bang she performed in and maybe that "truth" will fall to pieces. Everybody you see when you are watching porn is somebody's daughter or son. Everybody you see on the screen have been young girls and boys with their own dreams and expectations, and I'm pretty sure that none of them would have answered; "porn actor/actress" when asked what they dreamed about working with as a kid. I will conclude this part on porn with an extract from a story an ex porn actress has published. Since she is American I'll just keep the text as it was written and published on the internet:

"Sex-packed porn films featuring freshly-dyed blondes whose evocative eyes say "I want you" are quite possibly one of the greatest deceptions of all time. Trust me, I know. I did it all

the time and I did it for the lust of power and the love of money. I never liked sex. I never wanted sex and in fact I was more apt to spend time with Jack Daniels than some of the studs I was paid to "fake it" with. That's right none of us freshly-dyed blondes like doing porn. In fact, we hate it. We hate being touched by strangers who care nothing about us. We hate being degraded with their foul smells and sweaty bodies. Some women hate it so much you can hear them vomiting in the bathroom between scenes. But the porn industry wants YOU to think we porn actresses love sex. They want you to think we enjoy being degraded by all kinds of repulsive acts."

It doesn't get any clearer than this. Be sure you know what it is you're watching and be critical. To not let porn damage our senses or our bodies we have to be aware of the forces that are at hand. As they said in the popular series Hill Street Blues in the 80'ies: *"Hey, be careful out there!"* and make sure that you are controlling the porn and not the other way around.

And now, over to something completely different….

LOVE

What's happened to love? Has it gone out of fashion or become extinct? Sometimes that's how it feels when you look around, in society, when watching the news on TV, in the newspaper's headlines and seeing people's expressionless faces when they walk down the street either lost in their own minds or plugged in to a phone. But, when I Google the word "love" I get no less than **two billion eight hundred forty million hits!!!!** That beats both sex and porn put together. I'm so happy that it confirms my opinion that it is love, more than anything, we search for, wish for and live for.

To write about love as a subject is not that easy. Love is complex, to say the least. It exists in so many varieties and even if we try to differentiate love in various kinds of love, it is the same, it is unfathomable, limitless and most of the time quite magical. Love, just as other feelings, dreams, hopes and thoughts are nothing we can look at or touch, but we know that they exist anyway. We say that love lives in our hearts and those who can't love have closed their hearts. But when we love we feel it in our entire body, maybe primarily in our heart, but not one single cell is untouched by it. Love is what has inspired the making of so much music, lyrics, novels, movies, sculptures and plays and keeps on inspiring. When we fall in love the first time we are convinced that no one has ever felt this way before. It feels huge, powerful and breathtaking. The world becomes this beautiful place where food tastes better,

127

the colours are brighter, life is seen in a new light. Love awakens so many feelings and emotions inside us. Feelings that span all the way from the heat of passion to the deepest sorrow.

Today we don't talk so much about love; it is as if it's too hard and too uncomfortable to talk about. Apparently it's easier to discuss subjects like sex, violence, murders, catastrophes, cruelty and misery, at least if you judge by the output in the media. Love has been put in the backseat for quite some time now. Not in all areas and not for everybody, but I'm referring to the main stream of things. Maybe it's difficult because love is continually changing, it has no limits, it's fleeting and we want things to be easily examined the Newtonian way, we want to divide everything into little pieces, dissect it in order to understand it. Feelings overall seem to be more of a taboo to discuss today than sex was at the turn of the 20th century. Still, we know that a human being devoid of feelings is a deeply disturbed person and is among the scariest things we can imagine. At the same time, strangely enough, a cold blooded business man or some fearless adventurer is what many look up to and admire. Maybe that's because we all find it so confusing and bewildering to have all these feelings that we work so hard to keep hidden from others.

What surprises me the most is that when we talk about sex, which is in fact a physical expression for love; feelings in general are not mentioned. Porn will definitely have to take some of the blame for objectifying us so completely. What happens for many of us is that we can't be excited by porn, there is no credibility in seeing people without feelings that we can identify with, often not even sexual arousal, who perform acts that for most people have to involve powerful feelings to occur. The human body is not, and never will be, a completely mechanical device that we can use without consideration for the living being that feels, thinks and dreams, who lives inside it. And that shouldn't be what we strive for either.

In todays so called sexual education, the subject of sex is approached sort of as if it all was some kind of manual for a laptop. Press here, rub there, put this into that and see if it works! It's not that simple. We don't get sexually aroused just by someone touching the right places. Sex isn't an activity similar to the putting together of something we bought from IKEA. Something more than techniques is needed. Some say that our brains are our primary erogenous zone and that is to a large extent true, but without connection to our hearts, or love, the sexual experience simply becomes an expression for physical arousal and ejaculation, and why would we settle for that when there's so much more to experience?

As I've said before, we are all born as sexual and sensual beings. We have it inside but are not sexually mature until our brains and genitals have developed fully.

If we pick an apple too early, we know that it contains all the potential of a fully grown apple in terms of juiciness, sweetness and brown pits that can produce new apples. But when we take a bite of it we realize that in our haste to try it we have ruined all possibilities for that particular apple to grow, mature and become all that it was meant to be. It is important that we give ourselves and our children the opportunity to develop organically so that the natural maturing process isn't disturbed and we deprive ourselves of all the pleasures available when it comes to our bodies and sexuality. In order to develop into harmonious beings we need more than food, roof over our heads and clothes to keep us warm – we need love. That's not a romanticized notion but scientific facts. Experiments have been made regarding the development with and without love both as regards animals and humans. In Harry Harlow's famous experiment with Rhesus monkeys it is proven again and again how important love is for our psychological health and development. Those monkeys which were isolated and had no access to loving care developed deep psychological disturbances and several that had been in isolation and then were released went into such a severe shock when among other monkeys, they refused to eat and died a few days later.

The diagnose for those were "emotional anorexia". (Harlow also wrote an essay on his experiments that he called "The nature of love".) Love is vital for us, both during our childhood and during the rest of our lives. To many, the first infatuation gives them their first glimpse of the essence of love.

Our sensuality is developed through physical touch. Research shows that physical touch and contact increase our production of oxytocin, a hormone that generates a sense of calm, eases pain, decreases aggression and boosts our immune system. Children growing up with parents who are very tactile (no sexual innuendoes in this type of touch) have a more developed sense of understanding, confidence in and command of their own body as well as higher levels of empathy. In some kindergartens they teach small children how to massage each other to give them a better understanding of how it should feel to be touched in a comfortable way. There are baby massage classes where new mothers learn how to massage and touch their babies as well as senior homes where the elderly are given what is today given the term "tactile touch" since experiments have shown that we are healthier and happier if in physical contact with others. There is something slightly mechanical even in this, and it proves that we no longer trust our instincts and our innate knowledge in this area. Even commercial campaigns like "Give someone a hug today" proves that there is a lack of physical closeness that is free from sexual innuendo and I have to say I find it saddening that we find it so hard to show or give each other tenderness and love without either being paid for the services or alternatively having to be prompted by some commercial campaign or other.

It is a different kind of love to hug and be close to someone we "just" are fond of since that is a feeling which is free from sexual attraction and lust. But if we don't understand how much it increases our well-being to be in physical contact with another any other time in life, we completely and utterly get it when we're in love. We want to touch, hug and caress the object of our affection almost twenty-four hours a day. We want to hold their hands, stand beside, sleep next to, preferably wrapped around, we touch their hair, scratch their backs, kiss them, give them massages, anything to be in constant physical contact with the person who has awakened this strong feeling inside of us. As if we want to continually confirm that it is for real. The word "attraction" is given a whole new meaning and we feel just like magnets and iron filings, a power larger than ourselves draws us to this other person.

INFATUATION – FALLING IN LOVE

The romantic side of love or the infatuation primarily feels as if it has happened to us. That's how most describe it. We suddenly view this person, not only as a completely new individual, or someone who will pass through our lives. Without any warning a person can take on brand new qualities right before our eyes. We may even have had them in our lives for a longer time and have not seen them as anything else than friends, acquaintances, funny guys or something that makes us just see parts of them. Then one day when we talk to them, or dance with them or cook with them and a new sensation occurs, we feel hypnotized, fascinated, completely taken by this person. We have fallen in love. It could just as well happen on the subway, at our lunch restaurant, at the gym, we have this moment of sudden mind-blowing contact with another person we might not even have ever seen before, usually by catching someone's eye. We feel ourselves lost in someone's eyes for a while and life changes.

The eyes are the mirror of the soul it's said and this is true. We talk about "catching someone's eye", and there is something in this. The eyes and the look in them change when we fall in love and by "catching" the eye we also feel as if we've caught at least a part of their soul. (This is not saying that visually impaired people can't fall in love.) When you look into someone's eyes and suddenly see something new, something completely different from what you've seen before, it usually means that you have opened up to this person. Think about how you look at your loved ones, your kid, your mom and dad and compare that to how you look at people in the street, the bus driver, the shop attendant and you'll notice a difference. It's as if we can open our eyes for those we welcome into our lives and also close them to people who are not allowed entrance. For some reason we chose a specific person that we let catch our eye, to open up to, and more often than not it's worth our while, even if we don't fall in love every time we do it.

The romantic side of love, between man and woman, or between man and man, or woman and woman, is pretty much the same all over the world. We have different ways of describing the feelings but there is always an element of how heavenly we find this person, how intense the yearning is to spend all time with them and how the entire world seems to have changed when we are in love. Love has no age limit, no racial preference – that is really the most extraordinary aspect of love, it gives us a feeling of limitlessness and we feel bigger, stronger, more beautiful and more alive than we have ever thought possible. No matter how much researchers and scientists within biology and psychology want to analyse the infatuation or the falling in love-process, the fact remains, we don't consciously chose who we'll fall in love with or when it shall happen. We, as a race, humans that is, maybe can explain infatuation and love in scientific terms sometime in the future, but I don't think we'll ever be able to choose the object or timing. If we could, who wouldn't be constantly in love, and preferably with somebody who we'd know would reciprocate and who would always stay true?

But just as we have spent part of our lives being happily in love we have also, at least most of us, been in love with someone who didn't feel the same way or who after a very short period of time fell out of love while we were still in the powerful throws of infatuation. We have been tormented, longed for, questioned what, if anything, we could do to make them feel the same way again.

Being in love can be divided into two varieties. Some become so strongly attracted that they confuse it with being in love while others are capable of differentiating between strong attraction and being in love. And it's a common mistake to confuse them. They are both strong forces that affect us almost like some kind of happiness drug. In English you use *falling in love* but also *falling in lust* to describe the difference between them, where the one describes the phenomenon of being strongly drawn to another and wanting to have sex with them immediately and the other the surprising sensation of actually loving another person deeply wanting to be with them in every sense of the word even though soberly we realize that we really don't have a clue as to who this person really is. It's confusing to say the least, to fall in love. But so exhilarating.

Another person is suddenly seen as a whole new world to discover, every smile, every look, every touch feels as if you've discovered the meaning of life. For a true cynic there is nothing as silly as observing a person in love. They have no common sense to speak of, they smile continuously looking somewhat retarded and ridiculous, they find it hard to talk about anything but the object of their crush and they seem totally oblivious to the world around them. Love is blind is also a saying and we smile in recognition when we see the symptoms, but love isn't blind, but the emotional rush of an infatuation may well be. We are unable to see anything but the positive until the infatuation matures into love or slows down which can be a startling experience.

There are several theories about what an infatuation is and why it shows up and some of the more credible ones, apart from those who tell us about the pheromones and other chemical and/or neurological stuff, I believe are the thoughts around us all being born with a yearning for wholeness, and that this yearning often plays an important part in infatuation and love.

We all have a mix of masculine and feminine energies inside. In men it's usually the masculine principle that dominates, and vice versa with women. A man understands what it is like to be a man in a way no woman is able to understand fully. The same of course goes for women. This means that when we meet someone of the opposite sex we are offered an opportunity to both understand ourselves at a deeper level as well as understanding the other person in a way that is not equally true when we meet someone of the same sex or someone who is too similar to ourselves. To reach a deeper understanding for ourselves we need to relate to and get to know people we perceive as different. It gives us an opportunity to get in touch with feelings that may have been suppressed or blocked, that we haven't had the guts to face or even realized that we've harboured and thereby experience a deeper sense of wholeness within. The polarity between man and woman gives us, at least in theory, a possibility to get to know parts within ourselves that may have been underdeveloped or abandoned. The strong attraction between the sexes (apart from the purely physical attraction that is there for our procreation) could be this attraction or yearning to experience wholeness.

How many times haven't we seen a couple whose just fallen in love, happily describe how alike they think and are, some even want to dress alike. When we fall in love, we want to assimilate this person's feelings and experiences as our own and also share ours so that the sum total becomes larger than the parts. In this attempt to assimilate another person or become one with them, we have an amazing opportunity to grow and develop. The deeper we get to know each other's quirks and peculiarities, rhythms and likenesses in the infatuation phase the safer we feel. We create our own very special Universe where we feel we have a deep and meaningful contact and understand each other by simple means like looks, gestures, facial expressions and innuendos. We don't have to explain ourselves, we understand. Conversations and physical contact feel magical, amazing and spellbinding. In the infatuation phase everything is easy, our tolerance levels are higher than usual and our fascination with the other person increases our curiosity and acceptance. We believe we are the happiest people alive who have managed to find this very special person to fall in love with. If we succeed in getting to know each other properly and yet keep the warm, accepting and generous energy of love, the relationship will develop into real love. If we start to feel that the things that we first were fascinated by, most commonly our differences, begin to irritate us and we want to create a distance it usually doesn't take long before the glow of the infatuation goes out and what remains is nothing more than a pile of ashes.

But the very phase of infatuation creates in itself a will to love, a will to be tolerant, a will to understand, a will to accept and to like and it is this will that separates love in its more mature aspect from the infatuation. There is no act of will in the infatuation in the sense that we have to make an effort to go with the feelings, it kind of takes care of itself, sort of like sitting on the beach and letting the waves crash all over you. It is not until we decide to stay in the water and learn how to swim that will enters the picture. Fascination, attraction and passion can be there from the start, but love needs curiosity, patience, acceptance but also the courage and will to see the person as they truly are.

THE ROMANTIC RELATIONSHIP

When we have passed the infatuation and continue forward we have quite a bit of work to do. We start to discern reality again and therefore also clearly see the things we don't find so fascinating or cute. In the beginning you might have found it cute that she never was on time because she was so eager to look just right for you she always showed up late, out of breath and ready to serve you at least fifteen explanations as to why she was late. Now it's not that cute anymore and you have tried to make her understand that you don't like to be kept waiting. You find it disrespectful and see it as a lack of planning capabilities. The next time she is late you get angry and show it, you have your first fight or at least your first difference of opinion.

And this is the way it goes. In the "sobering phase" the pink cloud that was so pleasant to sit on dissolves and the clarity of our vision makes us wonder if this really is as fantastic as we first thought. We shift between visits back in the infatuation and the real world and it feels somewhat uncomfortable. We realize that this godlike creature which we've considered to be the only source of our happiness is in fact "just a mere human".

When two aware persons meet and fall in love, this phase doesn't constitute any real issue. But if we are not aware of how our emotions change and have our feet firmly planted in the ground, we start to blame our partner for the fact that we no longer feel as continually "high" and intoxicated any more. When we are unaware of our own emotional processes we often put the responsibility of our feelings on our partner. Some continue to do so their entire lives and life turns into an unending chase for new infatuations. New partners replace the old ones; the same pattern is repeated time after another and no development into a real relationship with lasting love ever occurs.

So how is it done? Well, hahahaha, that is the million dollar question. There is no quick fix for a successful romantic relationship because it takes time to get to know someone and also to get to know oneself properly, but there are elements and processes that are vital ingredients for a romantic relationship to last.

Communication

*"Occasionally in life there are those moments of unutterable fulfilment which cannot be completely explained by those symbols called words. Their meanings can only be articulated by the inaudible language of the heart."*Martin Luther King Jr

If we can't communicate with each other that is a problem. So much has been said on the subject of communication that sometimes it seems as if the words are more important than the feelings. But the words can't always be trusted. We don't put the same meaning into words even when using the same terms. Not even a term like "being faithful" means the same thing to all people. Some think that means that you can't have physical sex with anyone outside the relationship, somebody else thinks it's enough to kiss someone else to be unfaithful, a third might think that just dreaming about someone else is enough, some may find it acceptable that the person have sex with someone else as long as they don't lie about it....the varieties are many which is why it is so important that we are clear about what exactly it is we are saying. In the beginning of a relationship it's common to misunderstand each other, unnecessarily so just because you haven't found out how the other person's thesaurus is made out. It is therefore wise to prepare for the fact that it is very likely that some "language barriers" will occur even when you have the same nationality.

The clearer and more to the point we are, the better the communication. To be truthful is one of the key ingredients in any good communication. Just as commercials we have a tendency to embellish ourselves in order to not get dumped by that someone we feel attracted to. In the beginning we might agree if he or she for example claims that they like "open relationships as long as you're honest about it" even if we really don't feel the same way. Maybe we hope that this person will fall so deeply in love with us that he or she will change their mind and only want to be with us. The lie is not only about trying to trick them into believing we are in agreement, it's also self deception at a high level when we aren't clear about what we like and dislike. The truth always have a way of showing up and to make it easier on ourselves it's vitally important to first know what we like and as well to tell our partners, even if we're afraid we'll be abandoned or have a fight about it. The more truthful we are in detail, the easier we make it for our partners to understand what happens.

Gay and Kathlyn Hendricks have written many great books on relationships and they often talk about the importance of telling the "microscopic truth" to keep communication open and clear. What they say is that instead of blaming and accusing our partner for whatever we feel they have done wrong we talk about how we ourselves feel about it, think about it or experience something. Say for example that the person we live with tells us he or she wants to spend the weekend with old friends instead of us. We might want to say something like: "You always do what you want and just leave me to spend time with others, while I sit here and wait, you don't give a damn about me, you just go off and have fun. You're an inconsiderate jerk!" But if we really made an effort to say the microscopic truth it might come out something like this: "When you look that happy about spending the weekend away from me I feel scared that you no longer want to be with me or that you don't care for me as much as you used to. I really do want us both to be able to do stuff on our own, but I'm also afraid that you are going to have more fun and enjoy yourself more without me than with me." To tell your partner how it really feels for you makes it easier to react with kindness instead of defence.

It isn't that easy to communicate clearly. Most of us don't get much guidance in the how-to's when we grow up. We are taught how to say "It wasn't me, it was Joe who broke the vase". How many of you have heard a child say: "I broke the vase, but I'm so afraid that you are going to be cross with me so I'd rather lie and say it was Joe who did it. " We figure out that if we twist and tweak the truth we sometimes can avoid scolding or dislike. Sometimes it goes as far as to us tweaking the truth even within ourselves so that we avoid our own judgment and dislike.

Good communication doesn't have to mean a lot of communication or endless conversations day after day. What is true in so many other areas is true when it regards communication as well; quality – not quantity is what makes the difference. That's why it's so important that we have the self insights and knowledge, and enough courage, to be able to tell the truth.

Communication happens in so many more ways than words. We communicate all the time with our facial expressions, our body language and underlying emotions. Most people can tell if somebody says one thing but really means something else and it's when the whole package, that is, our words, our facial expression, tone of voice, body language and the feeling behind them match that our message truly hits the target.

The physical communication is extremely important in a relationship. Small touches that say "I care for you" stabilize the relationship and we have the pleasant feeling of belonging together. Our wellbeing increases by physical contact and to have your loved one's hand in yours feels both reassuring and nice. Our instincts tell us that it's good to show the world that we belong together, to tell the other "males and females" out there that this one is taken. But we also need to allow ourselves a lot of physical closeness in the privacy of our homes, even if that has nothing to do with the marking of turf.

Every touch doesn't have to be an invitation to sex, there's an absolute value in the closeness in whatever form it takes just as it is. We feel more relaxed when physically touched, partly because of what I wrote earlier with the release of oxytocin, but our emotions also tell us that everything is well when we are physically close to someone. I'm sure you can recognize the feeling when you are annoyed with someone or even really angry, and really don't feel like caressing them or giving them a hug. Physical intimacy often says more than a lengthy verbal explanation would. We communicate all the time, even when we're completely silent and it helps to be aware of how we communicate in all the other ways. A look can sometimes feel like a mortal stab, and at other times like an invitation to paradise. The tone of voice tells us if the person we are talking to is tired, happy, angry, irritated or sad. Just as important as it is to be aware of how we communicate and communicate well, it is important, and sometimes even more important, that we are able to listen and observe attentively.

"There's a reason to why we have two ears and one mouth" my teacher used to say in primary school. And I think there is. It's not wrong to listen more than we talk, we learn more and we are perceived as interesting and interested people. In a relationship listening is vital. How many times haven't we heard a husband complain that his wife doesn't understand him? Maybe she doesn't because she is too busy talking herself and never stops to listen. In relationships it is truly important to listen to your partner, especially when they are trying to explain how they feel regarding the relationship. The same way many women complain that their men don't take in the signals in different areas. For example, in bed. If you want to be the best lover your lover has ever had you need to be very observant on his/her signals when you make love. By being attentive you fairly easily notice what activities are more appreciated than others, if you should continue with what you are doing or if it's time to try something else. It's not that easy to describe all our likes and dislikes when it relates to sex, seduction and touch. It feels like giving instructions and that is really neither very sexy nor exciting.

Listening takes patience, we can't and shouldn't hurry our partner along when they try to convey something important. There are too many relationships that break just because the parties haven't taken the time to truly listen to each other. The technique where you repeat, in your own words, what you partner just said is an easy way to grease the wheels of communication. It's so frustrating to try to explain something over and over again and experience that the message has gone by unnoticed. A partner who is sure that he or she already knows what is about to be said and therefore interrupts the one talking, or a partner who keeps fidgeting or doing other stuff, who doesn't look the other in the eye or in other obvious ways shows that he or she is not listening closely are some of the most frustrating things when trying to communicate something important. We all can tell if our partner is interested or not and in a romantic relationship it serves you well to pay attention.

In a romantic relationship we sometimes believe we "know everything" about our partner, but when divorce or the break-up struck "like lightning from a clear blue sky" it can very well be that we haven't been as attentive as we should have or even interested enough to get that something might have been wrong. As a conclusion you could say that communication is about conveying who you are and what you feel, listen to what your loved one has to say and being attentive to the communication that comes out in other ways than in words. Also to keep asking and keep being curious when you feel that communication is stuck somehow and be generous in showing how much you appreciate and care for your partner. I have so far never met a woman who doesn't appreciate a spouse that leaves her love notes on the kitchen table, romantic text messages, a short phone call just to say "I love you" or shows her physically by giving her a big hug when coming home after work, a kiss for no reason when you are out shopping, an arm around her waist, a kiss on the neck when she does the dishes or just a kiss on the forehead when she feels tired and worn out. Communication in a romantic relationship is mainly about giving each other emotional support. To have someone to trust and lean on when the wind is cold is one of the best parts of being in a relationship. There are more than a million ways to show your partner that you love them and think of them, let your creativity flow!

Acceptance

To accept someone, just as they are, sounds so simple, but isn't. It's so much easier to accept someone we are not emotionally involved with just the way they are, but to accept ourselves or our loved one with flaws and defects is a completely different game. We resist what we don't like instead of accepting it for what it is and either let it be or try to change it. As soon as we resist something we don't like, the thing we don't want grows and seems to stare us in the face even more frequently than before. What we resist grows, becomes stronger and more inconvenient. If we are to go outside and it's pouring down when we want the sun to shine, we can chose to be upset about the rain, we can curse the weather and start several negative processes inside that make us feel out of sorts or we can accept the rain, bring an umbrella or a raincoat, wear rubber boots to keep our feet dry, and let the rain rain to its heart's content without letting it ruin our day.

Don't confuse resignation with acceptance, acceptance is a positive feeling, it feels good to accept something or someone while resignation feels negative and tiring. It's not until you've accepted something that you can change it, or change your reaction to it. If we take a person who is overweight for example who hasn't accepted the fact that they are overweight because they take in a lot more energy than they use up. I have heard several overweight persons complain that is unfair and that they put weight on just "looking at a Danish" or they tell you how they "only" ate this or that for lunch or dinner, how they have tried all the diets and exercise plans out there but "nothing works" and I've also seen the difference it makes when they accept things as they are. As long as they resist what is, that is in this context, that they eat too much and don't exercise enough, the weight just piles on, since they haven't accepted what causes it they can't either change the process. The resistance in itself also adds insult to injury since it makes them feel really bad about themselves because they are "powerless" and life is so unfair treating them this way. From the outside we clearly see what is happening, but when we find ourselves in a situation we resist, we are not as clear-sighted. To accept things as they are entails our letting go of the victim mentality. We stop blaming things outside ourselves and take on the responsibility for how we feel and how we live our lives.

When we accept someone or feel accepted, love is present. To accept doesn't mean that we approve it just means that we don't resist it. If I accept that my partner always is late I can chose to arrive fifteen minutes later to our appointments in order to not have to stand there and wait, I can use the time to run an errand or something since it can't very well come as a surprise that he's not on time, but if I continue to resist this fact and become upset and irritated every time and accuse him and thereby start yet another fight I have ensured that

146

whatever we met up to do is going to be tainted by those feelings. Acceptance shows that we always have a choice. We can choose to accept or we can choose to resist. To accept or at least nurture an accepting attitude is also a vital ingredient in a successful relationship.

A sense of humour

It's wonderful to have a romantic relationship where you laugh together, where you have the same sense of humour and also that you both have the ability to laugh at yourselves. Laughter can bring two people together but it can also keep people at a distance. The difference lies in the fact that some people use humour to get out of being sincere. It's as if they just can't refrain from coming up with a dry remark or some clown act when conversations turn serious. This is the type of humour that is used as a weapon to keep people at an arm's length and usually it's not charming for very long. It can't be humour at the expense of closeness but humour that is welcoming and warm. You know what I mean, there is always someone in our circle of acquaintances who is the "funny guy", who always have a sarcastic remark up their sleeves, who always strives to keep the conversation light and who in the long run still is seen as rather fun, but somehow also sort of one-dimensional and not so interesting. "Too much and too little can shame anything" is quite appropriate in this context as well.

It is however fantastic with people who have this intelligent sense of humour, that makes us laugh and who we share the laughter with. Laughter in itself is a release; it makes us open up to each other. When we laugh uncontrollably our defences are down and we therefore allow funny people into our lives more easily than others. But as always there is a balance that needs to be upheld. It's not supposed to be fun all the time, we don't want a non-stop comedian in our midst who doesn't understand when it's appropriate and when it's not to turn to humour. I have to confess that I have a weak spot for people with a great sense of humour, not the "practical joke" kind of humour, but people who make interesting observations and have a quick wit. I have even found myself falling in love just because they have managed to make me laugh uncontrollably. A person with this intelligent sense of humour doesn't need as much surface qualities to enchant the opposite sex. If we find someone funny we often find them charming as well, no matter what they look like. For me it has to be a sense of humour that is connected to this observational capacity, a person who has observed both himself and others and seen the humour in our behaviours who also has the ability to express that in ways that make you recognize yourself. Many stand-up comedians use exactly that. In a relationship it's also important to be able to observe yourself and at times laugh at yourself.

Too many of us take ourselves too seriously. We feel hurt, upset and insulted instead of laughing it off. Especially in romantic relationships. When among our friends we can be easy going and laugh at all sorts of stuff, but when we are with our partner we try to be somewhat "better" than otherwise which can have the effect that we become a more boring version of ourselves in our attempts to be the "perfect partner". This is especially true in the beginning of a relationship. We don't want to be perceived as ridiculous or silly, we want to be magically attractive, exciting and mysterious and that doesn't leave too much room for humour. It's something so refreshing and honest about a heartfelt laughter it makes us feel comfortable. To many it seems as if just this feeling of relaxation and comfort is somehow dangerous since it does also include a sense of closeness and when we are close to someone we might risk being exposed for who we are and it seems that that is exactly what we are trying to avoid when we take ourselves too seriously. All of us have illusions about ourselves that we want to keep up; we have a self image that we are comfortable with, sometimes no matter if it's really true or not. We can get stuck in our ideal self image to such an extent that we prioritize this vision of ourselves at the cost of a solid relationship.

Self-examination, that is, the ability to be able to look at yourself without trying to improve anything and accepting what you see, makes it unnecessary to fearfully stick to the illusion. When we make the illusion more important or more real than reality we become fearful since we on some level know that the illusion is in fact an illusion and it's really just a matter of time before it is revealed. If a person for example has the illusion about themselves that they always have an impeccable surface she/he might be admired to some extent because of their choice of clothing and their ironed, crisp and fresh look. Their safety consists of a uniform chosen for the day and as long as the uniform is impeccable they experience a sense of being in control or feel some form of self confidence. If this type of person experiences an incident, say her stockings get a run, the zipper breaks or their hem falls down, they lose their cool in a way that to others seem somewhat comical, even hysterical and unbalanced. The very thing they want to avoid at any cost has just happened and their masks crack and we can see the fear behind it. It takes a lot of energy to cover up your "flaws" which is why it's sometimes easier and gives you more credibility if you are open with them. This controlling need often looks comical to others. With a little self distance and self irony we can afford to allow the outward mask to crack open at times and even notice that the world doesn't stop turning because of it.

Laughter is a way to let go of control for a bit. A heartfelt laughter will come out as it is and when you try to control it the joy of it all has also been deadened. Sometimes laughter functions as a stress release, we start to giggle uncontrollably when it's completely inappropriate, often when we feel nervous about something. The surplus of nervous energy in our bodies is released thru the laughter.

To look at yourself and life with a sense of humour makes life easier both for yourself and for those you spend time with. In a relationship humour creates a higher level of tolerance and a more accepting environment. Not one of us is perfect and it helps if you just accept that and even see the humour in your own and other's attempts to reach perfection. Truth be told, no one wants to live with someone who is flawless, that would be like living with a robot.

This thing about showing our emotions in a non-controlled manner, in all areas, seems to be the one thing that makes people around us feel ill at ease and uncomfortable. But if we don't even dare to laugh uncontrollably there's a risk we won't dare to love uncontrollably either.

Being

Control seems to be the new "god" for many. Control and resistance are pretty much alike. If we control emotions and feelings they are suppressed and become stronger. With a too controlled person we sense that it's like being around a pressure cooker, there's a lot of turbulence below the surface and that might make us feel we have to tip-toe around them in fear of releasing whatever is brewing there. To be controlled is not the same as being calm and balanced. To be uncontrolled does not mean that you express all your emotions in a chaotic manner. If we, say, feel disgust with people who are obnoxious and aggressive, we can be sure that we are working hard at controlling or resisting our own feelings of aggression. We won't allow ourselves to behave in a way that awakens our own disgust when we see other people do it. The more we control or resist it, the angrier we get at those who are aggressive enough to take what is theirs. We might even become so good at controlling this feeling that we believe it's not in us. We can hold grudges, fret and gripe for hours and in that way completely darken our lives. Those who have been aggressive aren't suffering because you sit at home cursing them. This is the way all feelings and emotions function when we try to control or delete them from our lives and beings. Instead they become twisted and grow in strength, because the truth is, we are all capable of each and every feeling and emotion we see "out there" no matter how good we get at controlling them.

150

If you control an emotion you experience as negative it's very likely that you also control those feelings you would really like o feel in full. You want to control your anger and the effect is you can't feel joy as strongly. We don't need to act crazy because we don't control our feelings; it's more likely that when we allow our feelings to be felt (not necessarily expressed) without trying to control them we can act in a very balanced and agreeable manner.

It does take some work to have insight in and accept all our feelings but it's so worth it. I'm not saying that we should aim for an existence where we don't feel or try to achieve some sort of guru-like sublimity where we walk thru life with a quiet smile not reacting at all. No, what I'm after is that we overcome the fear of our emotions, see them as they are, accept them and in that way stop being victimized by our own emotional build-up and instead have the choice to give into those feelings and emotions that feel pleasurable.

Just being and refraining from disciplining yourself all the time is very relaxing. Life becomes hard when we resist it. One of my girl friends used to say "when you're sad – cry, when you're angry – scream and shout, when you're scared – tremble and when you're happy – laugh. First time I heard her say that I thought it sounded a bit *too* easy a life philosophy, even if it sounded very easy-going and relaxed as well. But that is really how simple it all is even if it's not always easy to practice it. The key to allowing your feelings to come and go as they please may not be that you necessarily express them all the time but that you notice them and allow them to be there without trying to change them. Feelings always have a message for you and if you just listen to it you have just received another piece of the puzzle that is you.

In love it's both easiest and hardest to just be. Love has a tendency to awaken all our feelings and also makes us fearful that we might lose what we've just found. Many of today's philosophers and gurus say there are really only two feelings – love and fear.

Either we react from fear or from love. With fear comes anger, envy, jealousy, controlling needs, irritation, stress, discontent and so on. With love comes generosity, acceptance, benevolence, joy, warmth, tenderness, tolerance and so on. No matter how you prefer to define feelings and the number of basic feelings, we all have them to get to know and learn how to handle. In order to feel deeply and have intimate relationships we need to have the courage to *just be* with other people. Many won't allow themselves to just be in any other circumstance than when they are alone. They might even think stuff like "if so and so really knew how I am he or she would never want to spend time with me" or something close to that. The fear of being "completely naked" with another being makes us feel vulnerable but my experience tells me that when we let go of our fears we also give love carte blanche to take us to new heights. When someone we love courageously tells us something that they haven't dared tell anyone else before, our love grows.

What I mean by "just being" in this context is that it can be, and most often is, nurturing to love to allow yourself to just be with the one you love. It doesn't have to be that you have some deep dark secret to disclose, it can just be to allow ourselves to be a bit boring at times. People have such a fear of being boring today or being perceived as being boring it's almost funny. But the thing is, we are not twenty-four hour amusement parks and no-one expects us to be. There is nothing more irritating that having a person close by who always tries to be funny and amusing, lively and interesting, it becomes strained and you can see with a person who has that as a primary personality, how stressed out they get when the "audience" doesn't applaud or cheer all the time   All you want to do is shake them and scream RELAX FOR A MINUTE - P L E A S E! It is ok to be boring at times; it's also ok to be quiet, earnest, sad, pensive, brooding and just in general not very sociable.

The greatest joy derived from just being is apart from the general love increase, a sense of being more relaxed in the relationship when we have sex. To be able to just be when we are involved in sexual activities makes us say yes to sudden novelties, dare to be playful and be infinitely more present with our darling than when we are busy trying to figure out how we look, how we are perceived, if our performance is up to par and other worried thoughts that come from our fear that he/she won't feel the earth move when we have sex. The playfulness and sense of exploration are ingredients which make our sex life as adventurous as it has the potential to be. When you are relaxed and let things be what they are, innocence returns.

Just like when we were kids and were absorbed by the play. We tried new stuff; we turned and twisted, dug and built and discovered new ways to play in the middle of play. When you make love to your partner and get in touch with this feeling of innocence, or that everything really is new, you might discover completely new things that your loved one appreciates. Every new person and body you will come in contact with contains more possibilities than you think. It's like exploring a new planet where every curve, every inch can represent a new avenue for pleasure.

Most of us get stuck in a rut, even when it relates to love and sex, areas which have endless creative potential. We do what we've always done and what has worked before. But why limit ourselves? Just as in the child's play it's not the presence of a lot of toys that make the play intriguing. We use what we find and let our creativity and fantasy take care of the rest.

When you let go of control and are present in the now, the physical act of making love becomes something new and surprisingly fabulous every time. We love more deeply, more passionately and openheartedly when we dare to let go for a while and just enjoy the ride that passion and love take us on.

Fantasy

"The gift of fantasy has meant more to me than my talent for absorbing knowledge."
Albert Einstein

Wise man, Mr Einstein. We all have our fantasy, not all of us use it, but it's there for anyone who feels up to it. We are raised to "not sit on a cloud" in some kind of fear that we'll become dreamers who never achieve anything, or that we won't be able to see the difference between fantasy and reality. Maybe the real fear of our fantasy is that we know that it's in our fantasies everything has its beginning. Our fantasy is creative. Something starts as a dream and becomes real. Someone said "if you can think it, you can do it" and if it hadn't been a fact that fantasy and/or creativity is what creates and changes the world, we wouldn't have had airplanes, cars, washing machines, computers, telephones, electrical light and all the rest either, since they are a result of someone taking their fantasies and dreams seriously.

When we are children we are more open to fantasy. We use it daily, to learn and to amuse ourselves. Children, and some of us grown-ups, have always felt fascinated by fairy tales about dragons, princesses, ghosts, wizards and other people with magical gifts, animals that can speak and everything else that exists in fairy land. As kids we live in a world where everything is possible. And why it would be viewed as grown-up to not believe that everything is possible I don't know, but that's how it is for many. Despite this we continue to read about the mysterious, we watch movies about fabulous adventures and dream our dreams. For some people dreams are "just" dreams and for others dreams are the starting point for a number of activities. With the assistance of our fantasy we can ignite our emotions. If we fantasize about something scary we feel anxious and fearful, we also react physically as if we were in real danger, our hearts beat faster, the adrenals produce adrenalin (in case we need to fight or flee) and we may feel our palms getting sweaty. If we on the other hand use our imagination to take us to the beach of a tropical island and get into that, we feel relaxed, happy, relieved and we can feel our bodies loosen up, we may smile and those good hormones that increase our well-being are produced at higher levels. When we just have fallen in love fantasies about the most recent encounter can be replayed in our minds and once again we experience those feelings of butterflies, happiness, excitement or whatever it was that occurred then.

We have all fantasized about and experienced a sexual encounter that results in our body responding as if it were actually having sex even if we find ourselves sitting in a car waiting for the lights to turn green. We think and fantasize daily about things that make us feel different ways irrespective of if we call it fantasizing or not. It has been said that we think approximately 50-60 thousand thoughts each day and that 95 percent of them are negative and/or repetitious. That's not putting our fantasies to good use especially when considering that our bodies and therefore our health are affected by what we think. So, it's a good idea to start observing where you're mind takes you during the day. If you don't believe that your thoughts affect your body you can try the following experiment:

Sit down in a comfortable position where you can be undisturbed for a few minutes. Take a couple of deep breaths. When you feel relaxed you imagine yourself being at home in your own kitchen. You see yourself opening your refrigerator door and look inside. You see a large bright yellow lemon on one of the shelves and you pick that up and close the door. When you see yourself holding the lemon in your hand you can feel the cool waxy surface against your skin. You put the lemon on the sink and take out a knife and cut the lemon in four cloves. The pulp is light yellow and you see how juicy it is. You then take one of cloves and watching it closely you see the juice dripping from it, you then slowly bring it closer to your mouth and take a deep bite into it, you feel the tart lemon juice stream into your mouth..

If you did this with just a bit of imagination you noticed how your mouth watered, even though you never actually bit into a lemon. Our brains cannot determine whether that was a focused thought or in fact reality. And the thought of biting into a lemon makes the brain send out signals through our bodies to prepare for the tart juice and makes sure that enough saliva is there to dilute it properly. In the same way all our thoughts produce a physical reaction. Not one single thought goes by without it having an effect on our body. You can choose to see it as a fantastic opportunity or as a flaw in your brain. No matter what you choose, the fact is, as is often said, we are not using any greater part of the capacity our brains have and that goes for our thinking capabilities as well as our imagination. The majority of us are instead used by our minds in the sense that we let it decide what to think and do not use it as the tool it really is. It's up to each and every one of us to choose whether we shall act and react as puppets on a string letting our minds do the pulling or if we want to be the ones that are in command.

In love and in the romantic relationship our fantasy is as an important ingredient to keep the relationship alive and interesting as is the air we breathe. When we find ourselves in a relationship where there is a lack of fantasy things rapidly get into a rut and a routine. Nothing new happens and we feel bored. If, in addition, we are not that self aware or take full responsibility for our own boredom it's easy that we blame our "boring" partner for the state of things.

Just because I talk about fantasy and imagination I'm not saying we have to think up mind-blowing activities like exotic travels, move to another house, repaint the old one or go bungee-jumping. It suffices to just use our imagination to think up small things that can delight and surprise our partner and also renew ourselves and the relationship in different ways. To get you started I'll jot down a few examples of what I'm referring to, some classics and some other stuff; use it for inspirational purposes, not as a rule:

Buy home food neither one of you have ever tasted (but make sure you have something you know you like at home as well just in case), cook dinner if it's always your partner who does that, write a personal letter to your partner and mail it to him/her, seduce your partner during the next sports show on TV (that is if you're the one who usually insist on watching it), light candles in the bedroom and give your partner a nice oil-massage (especially if you've never done that before), kiss your partner in a new way, make a date with your partner with a special "dress code", eat you entire dinner with your hands instead of cutlery, vacuum in sexy lingerie or naked, buy something nice for your partner to wear, be observant if your partner talks about something she/he dreams about or wishes and show them that you have noticed either by buying whatever it is or buy something that can be a part of making the dream come true, buy tickets to a concert or movie you both want to go to, take a walk in the middle of the night (preferably during summer maybe, though it can be nice when it's snowing as well), give your partner a gift without it being his/her birthday or any other anniversary, remember birthdays and anniversaries and make a BIG deal out of them, if your partner likes to be tickled or massaged, offer to do it without them asking for it, switch roles for an evening, he becomes she and she becomes he, pour a bubble bath with candles, music and bubbly wine – if you don't have a tub, have a shower together, decide that you shall be silent for a whole evening and try to communicate by facial expressions and your bodies instead…..

… you can make the list as long as you like, but what it really is about is doing something out of the ordinary, outside the comfort zone in a small way. Sometimes it's enough to just take the time, to for once ☺, really look our partner in the eyes and kiss them slowly with complete and utter presence and attention.

It's not possible to write a list that suits everyone; you know best what you might enjoy. Even that is possible to turn into an activity, to sit down and write down as many things as possible of these small things that you would appreciate and then have the list available if the inspiration hits a low. When we engage in new activities we feel more alive even it is small things like having something different for breakfast.

Imagination and fantasies can be used for so much more, but here I focus on the things that they can be used for in relation to the love life area. Love makes us dream and fantasize, we dream about the day we are going to meet HIM or HER and when we've met someone who meets the criteria we continue to fantasize about who this person really is, in the infatuation phase sometimes so intensively we don't even bother to look at the facts. We fantasize about how much this person loves us, how they will express it, if we are meant to live together, have kids, have the happily ever after ending and what that would be like. Sometimes our imagination leaves us with expectations that will never come true. Expectations are created in our imagination but can be harmful unless we are clear about them and/or communicate them to the person we want to share them with. To create expectations on what we want other people to do for us hardly ever come true since everyone has their own expectations and their own fantasies. That is why it's wiser to let our imaginations run wild when it relates to what we ourselves can do to make them real. Or, in a romantic relationship, we can tell each other about our dreams and fantasies to see if they correspond or if we can work together to make them come true.

Sexual fantasies are often at their best, as fantasies. If a woman for example dreams about being made love to by more than one man at the same time, her fantasy can be directed just as she wants it to be. She might imagine these men to be beautiful as Greek gods and all very much in love with her, all of them focusing on her pleasures, treating her like a goddess and naturally they would all know exactly what she likes and dislikes. In reality the scene may become completely different, it might instead become something much more like a gangbang, where the men are grubby and unattractive and don't care at all about what she wants, the whole thing could end up as a brutal and unpleasant experience. The definite advantage of keeping our sexual fantasies to our imagination is that we are the ones who decide exactly what they shall entail and include, how the people involved should look, what they are to say, what they are to feel and how they are going to act. To imagine yourself in a sexual situation with someone of the same sex might feel tempting, but to actually be there, touching their genitals, hear their voices and see their facial expressions might not be anything remotely like what we had pictured in our mind.

What we dream about sexually can give us glimpses of understanding about the feeling we are dreaming of to experience. For most of us fantasies are about a specific emotion and then I'm not just referring to excitement. We want to understand what lies beneath the excitement. The fantasies can be as far out as we want them to be, but that doesn't mean we are ready to face them or even want to experience them for real. Some who dream about a homosexual experience might fear they are closet gays, but more often than not it's about completely other things than that. Women might dream about other women because they yearn for a more sensual, slow and tender kind of sexual activity than they've experienced with men. A man who dreams about other men might want to experience sex where he can turn over the responsibility and not be the one having to take the initiative. You might think that this describes and even emphasizes the traditional or conventional thoughts around male and female sexuality and it might. But even if we do change, it is still more common that men are expected to initiate sex while women accept or decline. It's also so that a larger part of the female population, approach sex in a more slow and sensual manner than the male population. My interpretation here is just suggestions, not the TRUTH, etched in stone. The varieties are many and if we are alert and honest in our introspection we will surely realize what makes the fantasy so alluring. But the same way that we create expectations that won't come true and we feel disappointed, our sexual fantasies could have even worse outcomes if we try them with strangers in the real world.

Another advantage of using our fantasies is that it can be viewed as "safe sex", we won't for example catch a sexually transmitted disease by fantasizing about someone. Our fantasies can only damage if they create a distance to our loved one, to our own emotions or create an obsessive need. But the wonderful thing about it all is that we actually can experience everything we ever dreamed of even if it is inside our own minds since our brains create both feelings and physical sensations that go with the experience. It is however an even greater blessing when we can share our fantasies with someone we trust and love, who will assist us in the way that they do share it with us and do what they can to take part or act out the scenario. The deeper the love we feel, the greater the possibility to take part in and give our partners the experiences they've dreamed of in an accepting and playful way.

Love works in some aspects like a muscle, the more we use it the stronger it gets. Apart from those moments when we fall head over heels in love and feel that love just sweeps us off our feet, love is always a choice we have. To chose love takes practice and we don't become accomplished lovers in fifteen minutes. With "accomplished lovers" I am not referring to romantic seducers, I mean persons who have a great capacity for love. The advantage with practicing love is that the more love we feel, the better we feel and the more love we also seem to receive. As with anything else, what we focus on expands. How do we practice focusing on love?

Well, think about everything you already do love. Your children, your spouse, your siblings, your parents, grandparents, pets, soccer team, favourite song, favourite food, TV-series....we all love something or someone. Apart from the personal love we can love animals, plants, mountains, nature, peace, meditation, heaven, the oceans and the woods. Our love can be awakened in so many different ways and by so many different activities. On TV we've seen charity events and events where the objective is to raise money for different causes. These events show that there is a whole lot of love out there, a lot of generosity and warmth and it seems all that is needed is something to prod them in to gushing. Why it takes an event on TV to get in touch with these feelings of generosity and love I don't know but it is in any way really inspiring to see that so many are moved to tears, generously share their wealth and time and are courageous enough to show their love. In these kinds of events you can see how love as a force, as an energy, grows during these nights. We feel we're part of something bigger, we feel warm inside when we see that love is out there. It feels completely natural to help those who are suffering

When we feel this kind of love it often spills over into other areas as well and we view our near and dear ones with a greater sense of love than usual. We might feel a great sense of gratitude for everything we have that makes us willing to share. We need constant reminders on how important love is since we seem to forget all about it from time to time. One exercise that is usually very efficient to increase the presence of love in our lives is to take a moment each night before going to bed, to write down or at least make a mental list of everything we are grateful for in our lives. It can be about things that have happened during the day, there's always some small thing that has been good, maybe something as small as you were in time to catch the bus without running, someone smiled at you when you were waiting at the bank, a colleague said something kind, you had a great lunch – anything that you feel grateful for. Then there's always all the stuff that we take for granted, or maybe we don't take it for granted, but we forget to be grateful for it. The fact that you have a home and roof over your head, you have a job (that's something to REALLY be grateful for these days), you have friends, kids, sweet neighbours, a body that functions, your plants are healthy and thriving, you have food in the fridge, you see, hear, sense, that the sun rises in the morning and all the other stuff that we at times lose sight of.

When we are in touch with our innate feelings of love and gratitude this way, their presence grow to other hours of the day as well. When we constantly remind ourselves about the things we love and feel grateful for we begin to experience that there's a lot of it. Those persons, animals, activities and things we send a grateful thought to before the Sandman arrives at night, become yet another reminder when we see them in real life the day after.

THE LOVE OF OUR CHILDREN

"Mothering cannot be bought or sold, or reproduced by the marketplace. But caring can." Robert Manne

Motherly love has always been considered something out of the ordinary. As a mother myself I can assure you it is a quality of love that I wasn't really prepared for. There are testimonials on how mothers carry out next to miraculous tasks when their children have been in dangerous situations. The most commonly known is the one where a mother, without any other assistance, managed to lift a car from her child. That's a substantial feat. We have an instinct to protect our young. This instinct which varies in strength with different people can makes us run into a house on fire, dive into swirling water or any other thing that we normally wouldn't do even if we had a gun to our head. This instinctive love, because it is love, has an exceptional power and we accept it as something very natural.

It makes us put somebody else's needs before our own and even someone else's life before our own and we do it without thinking. I really wish everybody at least once in their life was blessed with the experience of this feeling, it makes us mature, we mature in love. We know that we can be as close to completely unselfish as is possible (because even if it's true that we are willing to protect this small creature it is also true that we love it so much we don't want to lose it and therefore you could consider it as a selfish act). Later on when this baby

163

starts to stand on their own two feet and develop a will of their own the previously constant presence of this protective instinct diminishes to the extent that they become self-sufficient. But no matter how old they get, the instinct is awakened when needed, and that is as it should be.

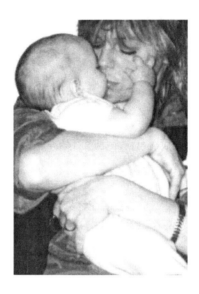

We claim that we love our kids and no one questions that and still there are so many kids who grow up today neither feeling loved nor safe. It is obvious that we cannot count on the instinctive love to suffice to create secure and balanced grown-ups. When the children grow up and become the individuals they're meant to be we also have to love them "voluntarily", that is, we need to consciously give them love which doesn't just give them the bare minimum of a roof over their heads and sufficient nourishment. The older they get, the more we have to improve our ability to show them love. If you compare it to the infatuation phase, which is comparable to when they're just babies, love is automatic almost. But, when they are older they need the love just as much or even more. According to research we are very much formed during the ages between birth and six years of age. Our senses have not developed fully and we do not have the critical ability which means we function more or less like tape recorders. We watch, listen and record everything we see, hear and experience as TRUE, and this programming can affect us for the rest of our lives especially if we are unaware of the program that sits there in our subconscious and is re-played every time we encounter something that triggers it.

When we are small beliefs and assumptions are formed on how love is given, how love looks, what love is and how a relationship between adults "is supposed to be". Since so very few of us have parents who are truly skilled most kids carry programs which may be neither efficient nor true. If we have parents or caregivers who do not give us love unless we have "performed" properly we find it hard to believe that anyone could love us just the way we are, even if we intellectually agree that it shouldn't be so. We keep trying to coax others to get the love we need. How many can't recognize themselves in thoughts like you want to be "the sexiest", "the best-looking", "the best cook", "the funniest" or whatever else we believe is what it takes to get someone to fall in love with us. As long as we do it and are aware that the reason for doing it is to delight, surprise or give the other a great experience it is alright. It is when we expect the result to be that we receive love that we feel devastated, disappointed and feel miserable when no love shows up. I think most of us have experience someone who is so willing to please that we can see them squirm just to get approval. Someone, I think it was Oprah, said that the need for approval or willingness to please has become one of the newest most widespread diseases and I'm inclined to agree.

This is why it is so important that we are aware of how we program our kids, that we avoid praising them only because they have performed a task well and instead give them love always, no matter what. Giving them love doesn't mean that we approve of everything they do, behaviours that are detrimental or damaging shouldn't be condoned, but we shouldn't either threaten to take our love away when they make mistakes. As parents we need to be wiser than our kids and supply them with the best possible conditions so they can

165

grow up to be loving and harmonious adults. Most parents do the best they can, and that is great, but today we know so much more about how we develop and how it affects us later in life and it can't hurt to find out more about how we can improve our parenting skills. It would be so liberating to not ever again have to hear "my dad used to spank me with a belt when I had done something wrong and that worked fine for me" from grown-ups when asked on their views on parenting. No matter whether it has damaged or contributed to an inefficient behaviour or blocks that are obvious, it's a no brainer to understand how a small child feels, being completely powerless, when the person who is supposedly the source of love, protection, care and warmth suddenly takes on this scary, painful and even dangerous character. I don't know what you think about that, but to me it can't be something that generates love and a loving behaviour.

Love is something we can give endlessly of without fearing that our kids will be spoilt, it's not by loving our kids they become spoiled, only if we define love incorrectly. Love isn't always saying "yes" to them, love is to show them that they always are treasured and that they can trust that they are safe, have guidance and are protected by us as parents. That they can count on the fact that we will be there, we love them and welcome them even if we at times don't approve of their behaviour. Think about that the next time you feel annoyed, before you explode, think about if there is a way to yell at the behaviour and not your teenager, rather say; "I really feel irritated when you don't clean up after yourself" than "you're so sloppy and lazy you drive me crazy". It's a huge difference between receiving scolding and criticisms for something you have done than for who you are. The fewer "you are"-messages in anger the better.

A stubborn teenager isn't always as easy to love as a baby. But a teenager, who is going thru puberty and all the other stuff that is so difficult that you have to go thru during your teen years, needs giant heaps of love. So many young people feel depressed today because they feel a lack of love and also a lack of skills in the art of handling their emotions. It is scary to hear that suicides are on the rise among teenagers and young adults, that they injure themselves by self-mutilation, anorexia, bulimia and other destructive behaviours when so much of it could have been avoided if we grown-ups had been better at love. Now you think that I am over-simplifying these problems, and I am aware of that.

I'm not trying to lay guilt on all parents with troubled teenagers. I know it's not that easy and even if you think you do everything and more it's not always enough. I'm just saying that if we are generous with love they will be better equipped to stand strong and not fall even if reality seems brutal at times. Young people are going thru all the things we have gone thru and in today's society maybe ten times as much. I'm sure you can recall how stressful it was to suddenly become "of age", fall in love for the first time, have all these feelings inside you haven't asked for, see society's ideals and images to live up to, decide what to do for a living and trying to get a place of your own. THE FUTURE is suddenly filled with insecurity and fear; will our bodies ever develop into that gorgeous image we see in the commercials, will we ever have a really loving relationship, will be finish school, will we have good enough grades, will we find a job, and so on and so on... Like baby birds suddenly kicked out of the nest they are expected to fly and it's not always certain that their wings will carry them.

All generations have gone thru puberty and completely easy and pain free it isn't. But with today's media governed expectations on how life will develop it's even harder. These expectations are in direct opposite to how reality is for the majority. The teen generation has to deal with so much more than finding themselves inside bodies that change and both become rather uncomfortable and not looking anywhere close to what we want them to, they get bombarded with messages on how a "gorgeous guy" or a "gorgeous girl" is SUPPOSED to look. Every waking hour they get impressed by these images and the chances for their bodies to become as exquisite works of art, that they meet MR/MRS Right who is a champion in love, have a sex life they can write biographies about before they've turned 20, have a job where they make more money than mom and dad, an apartment to die for and a huge social network of really fantastic and loyal friends they can travel the word and party with, is to put it mildly, microscopically small. Life isn't only a dance on roses and when we believe it is the fall into reality can be almost impossible to recover from.

Today's kids are stimulated from the day they are born (baby swimming, baby massages, baby dancing) up to their teens with schools, leisure activities, their cell phones, MSN, Facebook, TV, Youtube and movies. It's no wonder they become so used to a constant flow of activities that distract them so much that they almost fall into a depressive coma when they are subject to "BEING BORED". It's as if we started a race for our kids and are terrified that they should be - bored. But it's not until we get some down time, a moment of quiet that we really can connect to each other and even ourselves. That's not possible as long as all the distractions are up and running. To reach the depth and to reach anyone else we have to have the courage to be quiet, to refrain from distractions and focus on giving each other time when we simply *are* together. That's when we realize that love is always there beneath the surface and that this feeling of something missing only grows stronger when we are too busy chasing around like cats after their tails. That's when we realize that happiness or love or wellbeing can be likened to a cat's tail, when we chase it it's always beyond reach but when we just walk about minding our own business, it follows us wherever we go.

The need for approval and affirmation that has arisen from this development and that people seek in all the wrong places is relatively easy to satisfy when it regards our children. It's as easy as seeing them, really seeing them, and taking the time to listen. Let them figure out what to do, let them tell you about their thoughts about their day, their friends, their wishes and dreams without interrupting or correcting, let them sit close to you, look them in the eyes and LISTEN!!! I have said this before but repetition is good. LISTEN! To listen means that you refrain from figuring out solutions or advice on what is said until asked, it will take you further than you think to just listen.

LOVE OF SPORTS

All sport freaks know what I talk about here. The love we feel for a soccer team, any sports club or a specific sport is a common way to channel our love and our enthusiasm. Love for a team gives so many people a feeling of fellowship, a feeling of being part of something greater and also creates a sense of connectedness. The team or the club becomes "mine" and I rejoice when they are successful and suffer with them when not. This is often about a feeling of love that contains loyalty, the collective power of sharing this love and also a certain parental protection and will to share responsibility for the team. Love comes in all sort of shapes and even if we don't think "love" when we hear a baseball or hockey fan talk about the latest game, it's is an aspect of love that is present. Dedication is an aspect of love and anyone who has been dedicated to a cause or to a person can confirm that. We are moved by it, we are on fire; we spend a lot of time with it just the same way as when we are truly in love with someone.

Unfortunately many of those who have called themselves "devout sports lovers" are the type of person you today feel somewhat ambivalent towards. This exact type of "lovers" in connection with sports are no longer associated to love. In their dedication to the club many become aggressive, belligerent and combative. When this happens the devotion becomes somewhat fanatic and instead of being joyous moments the games become miniature combat zones where assaults and violence occur. When the driving force behind the dedication is tainted by malicious joy, envy and struggle we have strayed a long way away from being lovers.

Many become so exaggeratedly "dedicated" that they seem to put their interest for sports above everything else. Some people are what I call sports loonies, and with that I mean those who are interested in all kinds of sports no matter if it's fencing or the World Championships in hockey. This is basically the same as being addicted. They think that the whole day is ruined if they miss some sport event and sports are always more important than non-sports. At those unfortunate times when this type of person is involved in a relationship with someone who is not a sports loon it seldom ends well, because just like the nylon fetishist was asked, the sports loon will sooner or later be asked "who do you love the most, me or sports?". This is however not to be termed fetishism since this interest in no way is of a sexual nature, but there are many similarities in the exaggerated way they are dedicated to their thing becomes a refuge and replaces important things like intimacy, connectedness and openness towards other people, sometimes even towards those they claim to love including their children.

When I watch sports on TV, I can on the one hand understand the rush of joy, the excitement and the powerful feeling of being one of thousands of people cheering for the same thing and on the other hand I can feel a slight apprehension when large masses of people react as one single person. It looks as if many completely lose their common sense and just go along with the mass hypnosis. If something goes wrong it can change the entire energy from being energetic, joyous and inspiring to completely destructive and hurtful. I feel an enormous respect for the force that comes into action when we are gathered in large numbers. We have seen how scary it gets when panic breaks out and people without thinking trample each other to death. Sometimes it's enough with one bad apple to turn an entire crowd. To cheer for a team by howling and slapping each other on the back like a bunch of happy baboons is one thing, but to beat one of the opposing team supporters to a pulp in the heat of the moment is of course something completely different.

The odd thing is also that you don't see this type of love gone bad in individual sports events like athletics, swimming and such and even though it is World Championships and other types of big events between different countries where you would think the country would be thought of as the team it's rare to see anger flare up in the galleries. Then it seems to be possible to keep the interest, the dedication or the love for the sports to something with a great sense of sportsmanship and very positive. We become moved to tears when we see an athlete who has performed something outstanding climb up the podium and we feel very proud when one of our countrymen has achieved something spectacular. It is a great feeling to be that devoted or dedicated to something but necessary to not lose our common sense to the extent that our dedication which started out as feeling of love and genuine interest become tainted by aggression and hate.

THE LOVE OF OUR PETS

During 2005 a study was made that showed that in over 40% of the Swedish households there is a dog or a cat. That number is surely higher especially after Paris Hilton made the dog into an accessory. Nevertheless the love we feel for our pets is generally both strong and beautiful. We see a kitten or a pup and our hearts overflow when we see how helpless and cute they are. It doesn't take much effort to fall in love with a kitten or a pup, and that is exactly what happens. The infatuation and delight usually grows into a solid love. We view our pets as family members; some see them as their "kids" or their best friend. We can lavish our pets with unlimited love, they don't abandon us, they aren't critical, they never hurt our feelings, we don't need to make an effort to have them be there for us with their warm small or large bodies. No cat or dog will back away just because you haven't put your makeup on or taken a shower, they don't find us unattractive when we lie in bed with a runny nose and feverish eyes, we can sense that they love us unconditionally. And they do. We never have to risk hearing that we are too clingy from a dog; they will come every time we call their names and will wag their tails just as appreciatively and happily every time we hold up the ball and pretend to throw it. We say that there are "cat" people and "dog" people, that is, people who prefer one to the other. The cat people claim they love cats because they find their independence attractive and the fact that cats seem to believe that they are your landlords and you are just a houseguest, while dog people say they love dogs since they are forever loyal and always show you appreciation. Either way, our pets give us a feeling of never being lonely, of having a companion that has no expectations on our behaviour or looks.

The undemanding nature (apart from the fact that you have to walk your dog, clean the litter box and feed them) is something we can learn from. To be loved without a lot of demands for or expectations of certain specific performances feels great. It is however very much easier to feel this type of unconditional love towards a pet than another human being. Of course we can get annoyed when they scratch our furniture or bark every time the mailman passes by, but we soon forget when they come purring or just sit there and watch us with their kind and wise eyes.

It is a known fact that we experience an increased wellbeing both physically and emotionally when we spend time with our pets. To sit with a cat in your lap and pet it has shown very positive effects on blood pressure, hormone levels and peace of mind. Animals are also used in different types of therapies for kids who have difficulties dealing with life. When they get to know, care for and learn about animals their understanding of themselves and other processes in their environment deepens. It's also very good for your self-esteem to be responsible for another living being, irrespective if it's large or small.

Animals make us laugh, they do funny stuff, they are what they are and don't try to be anything else. We would find it ludicrous if we found out that a dog had low self-esteem because he wanted to be a cat! Still we, in our human and "sophisticated" world have created so many rules and regulations for our own behaviour that we control ourselves to the degree that our authentic and natural self almost never get unleashed. We are filled with hang-ups and develop neurotic behaviours because we want to be something we're not. We even pay large sums of money and suffer thru surgery to look different, we have anxiety attacks because we don't look like Photoshopped artists and run around like crazy to get at least one

Prada handbag or something else that will prove that we're cool enough. It makes me wonder whether we are in fact the highest developed race at least in this context.

It does feel liberating to spend time with someone who is completely free of affectation and with whom we also can stop posing for a while. That quality is truly an aspect of love and at times it's beneficial to reflect on how much unconditional love we are capable of when it regards our friends or our lovers.

This semi-new thing with dressing up your dogs in designer's clothes and jewellery must seem utterly ridiculous to most people. To hear these dog owners focus on the different outfits for their dog and at the same time see those poor creatures, who obviously doesn't think it's a blast to run around and look laughable, make me wonder how their owners view them. Do they have any respect for the fact that this is an animal, a living being, and not just their latest toy? On the one hand they treat their dogs as babies on the other as a thing to be exhibited to show the world what a "creative and hip" person who owns it. They talk to the dog in an artificial and mannered way and everything normal and natural about the dog is no longer present. In my eyes this is a completely backwards way to try and "humanify" the dog since the clothes don't make it human; it "de-dogs" it instead so it's neither dog nor human.

Animals are beings with feelings and needs. Just like us humans animals feel both fear and love and I'm sure some of the nuances in between. A frightened dog shows aggression because it feels afraid or unsafe, just like a fearful human being does. So in that respect we are already alike. To force them to wear clothes and jewellery is on the other hand completely unnatural for a dog and has nothing to do with the owner's love for it. It's only about the owner wanting to create or uphold an illusion about him- or herself in the same way we use cars or other fashion- or status symbols to achieve this. Usually you can tell what level of insecurity the person is at by observing the intensity with which they identify with the stuff.

It's even more absurd when "civilized" society at the same time have tried to instil the notion that animals do not have feelings like we do and there is therefore no need to treat them as if they did, that is with dignity and respect. Most likely to keep the meat-, egg- and milk production efficient and profitable. To on the one hand see animals the owner's claim will be "upset" if they have the wrong outfit on, and on the other see animals kicked, herded and under painful circumstances be brought to slaughter doesn't only show the inconsistency in our view of animals, but it also seems completely insane (in both extremes). The reason we feel upset when we see animals mistreated is that we do know that they are living creatures, not so different from ourselves.

Love is used for so many strange phenomena that when looked at a bit more closely really don't have anything to do with love. The kind of love that animals represent and show us, both pets that we mostly keep for the love of them, but also the animals we put to work,

178

like horses, hens, cows, goats and others, deserve our absolute respect and love. We don't have all the answers as to how animals function, feel and maybe even think, far from it, and to just out of laziness chose to see them just as a response to a need, is not only cruel but also inhuman and wrong. Animals have more to give and teach us than just companionship and edible products if we only open our eyes with a sense of reverence and humility.

For many years now we have for example been able to read about the healing abilities of dolphins, both out in the wild as well as in captivity. There are numerous different programs and projects that offer autistic children or retarded children and grown-ups the possibility to swim with dolphins and they leave happier, healthier and more verbal. Dogs have proven to be able to be the eyes for blind or vision impaired people but have also proven to be of assistance for persons with severe epilepsy since they can sense a seizure coming on and therefore lead the person to safety or in different ways attract attention so that the person can prepare for their own safety. We know that animals perceive other signals than we are capable of with our vision and hearing, but also in other ways that we haven't been able to really explain yet. We have both likenesses and differences but just as it is true when discussing racism that it might be easier to love and understand someone who is like us, it can be a lot more enriching to extend our capacity for love to those who have slightly different qualities. Our connection and contact with animals teach us a respect for all life forms (humans, animals and plants) and also show us the importance of respecting all life if we want to survive on this planet.

THE LOVE OF IT ALL

The universal or divine love that includes an awe for life as it is, the earth, space – everything, is the kind of love that transcends the mundane at the same time as it is the kind of love that truly gives us the possibility to experience all the small miracles that happen in our day to day life. That love is in itself a miracle since it awakens the good qualities in all of us. The divine love or spirituality has had a bit of a revival thru "New Age". We talk about new age today as if it was something new, something rather fuzzy, lacking credibility. And, I agree, there are quite a few things that are labelled new age, that are dubious, but new age in itself is really a compilation of philosophies, wisdom and thoughts that are ancient. The term new age, refers to the Aquarian Age – that is year 2000 – 4000. But there really isn't that much new to new age. What is new is that we today have the possibility to scientifically test certain theories and that has shown that some of the thoughts or spiritual wisdom that before couldn't be proven or which didn't have any "solidity" now has proven true. In everything that is included in the term there is a common denominator and that is a higher power or God if you like.

We can't explain everything – yet, and maybe that is a good thing. Even if science today can describe the chemical and biological processes that take place in different areas there is also always a few questions that remain. Me, I still think it's miraculous that I can just turn a switch that makes the lights go on, or get the electrical power to turn on a hairdryer for example, even if I did study physics in school. It's also connected with a sense of wonder when I see nature awaken after a long winter, when I stand on the shore and watch the ocean's waves continuously roll, when I a clear summer's night look up to the sky and try to fathom that it goes on forever, or that the tiny specks of stars that I see can be larger than the earth, when I at dawn see the sun rise on the horizon and everything is still except the birds, or when I try to really grasp that my daughter is the result of something as tiny as a sperm and an egg and that she has in fact grown inside my body..... Even if I very clearly remember what it was like to be pregnant, how it felt to give birth to her, how tiny she was and how she has now grown into a the woman she is today, it still feels slightly unbelievable at some level.

The wonders of nature are something that just are there, it's not our endeavours that have created them, they are already created and continue to be created all the time. We want explanations on everything and curiosity and the enthusiasm for exploration are in most areas good things. But they can turn into a need for control that will suffocate our zest for life and the joy of living. A too strong need to control life makes us lose respect for it. Even if we know for certain that it takes a sperm and an egg to produce a child we still can't control when and if it really will happen. Couples that go through IVF, where all conditions, in scientific terms, are perfect, don't always succeed. There is always that uncertainty that makes us scratch our heads and wonder "why"? This urge to control life is most likely there because we so don't want to die. But too many live their lives in a condition that more resembles a living dead, just because they let this fear dull the experience. And fear is, no matter how you look at it, the opposite of love.

Even if you don't aim any higher than to feel better, it can be beneficial to explore the experience of the divine, spiritual or universal love. When you do get in touch with the feeling you experience calm, a sense of awe and trust, which make the stress of all the little things in life, dissipate for a while. The body and the mind get to rest and thereby heal or restore themselves. How to get in touch with the feeling of universal love is different from person to person. For some a quiet walk in the woods can suffice, to sit down by a lake or just sit on the grass and see it grow. You can learn how to meditate and silence your mind so that you get in touch with your innermost self, and I'm not referring to your liver or your intestines, but your innermost energy or feeling. When the mind quiets down you can feel worry and stress dissolving. That's usually the time when we are at our most creative and have those great ideas. If they are the result of chemical/biological processes or spring from something bigger maybe isn't what we need to focus on. I'm sure you have experienced that you've spent several hours trying to figure something out or remembering something, it could be a name or a solution to a problem, and suddenly it dawns on you when you take a shower, or do the dishes or take a walk. When we engage in activities that don't necessarily take up that much thought processes, it's as if we open the doors and just let the solution or thought in that we spent the whole day trying to figure out. It is when we force, control and manipulate that our lives get stuck. Simplified it looks as if all we need to do is let go and relax to find out what to do next.

The spiritual love teaches us just that, to let go, to realise that life goes on even if we relax for a few minutes. We are not on our own the creators of the Universe and the world won't collapse if we let go of control for a while. The opposite is even more true, our private and personal universes find a way to balance themselves when we, at least from time to time, stop trying to figure everything out and control everything. It's also good to realize the fruitlessness of trying to hurry life up. If you plant a carrot seed in a pot and watch the small sprout in the black soil, you need to wait, water and nurture the sprout for it to grow into a carrot. If you start to pull at the sprout in your impatience for it to grow all you will have is a pot of soil. Sometimes we have to let life control what happens in order for it to work. There is this short story on how our eagerness to control and our fear can stop us from finding the solution to a problem:

A man was walking along a path in the woods when suddenly he tripped on a branch and fell into a deep hole. He landed at the bottom and saw to his dismay that water seeped out through an opening by the floor. He could see in his mind's eye how he would drown if he didn't find a quick way to get out of the hole. He tried to climb and use the roots or get a grip somewhere in the mud but fell down to the bottom each time. He tried to stuff the opening where the water seeped in with pebbles to stop the water but each time the mud dissolved and the water poured in with more force. In his panic he couldn't see any solution to his situation. Finally he gave up, sat down at the bottom of the hole and let the water soak him. At that moment he realized how he would get out of the hole. He made the opening for the water bigger and saw the water pour in, and then he calmly waited for the water to fill the hole and he was effortlessly carried up all the way to get out.

So many things in life do take care of themselves; if we don't resist them. We have bodies that take care of the digestive processes, the blood circulation, breathing and which also tell us when we are hungry, tired, angry or happy. Nature grows and rests and seasons come and go without us interfering, and the earth continues to turn on its axel without our assistance. We would find it silly to hear someone say they were constantly worried that the sun wouldn't rise the next day, or if he or she couldn't sleep because they thought they were responsible for that. We know that we have to accept the forces of nature, we can learn how they function and try to protect ourselves from them when necessary, but to be constantly worried about them would be to waste our life away.

To me, it's absolutely so that there is some kind of intelligence that have created everything so wisely. If that intelligence is to be called God or not, really isn't important. Life as it is and as we see it in nature is so wisely arranged that it keeps astonishing me. Not only all the functions in all the eco-systems make me filled with respect, the beauty of it all is so exquisite and shows such an abundant creativity that it's impossible to top no matter what works of art, music or other creations us humans have been able to produce.

No matter how you look at it, we haven't created the earth or life. If that in itself proves that there is a God I can't answer, but I can sense the goodness in the love and wonderment I feel for the whole of creation. When I'm in touch with this love I feel both very small and very safe at the same time as I get a feeling of crystal clarity. The clarity gives me a certainty that the life we are given is possible to live in a wonderful way if we live in love and respect for all living things. The thoughts and philosophies that we find at the indigenous people of the US, the Indians, in Asian cultures, lie very close to my perception of spiritual love. It's always difficult to find words for these grand emotions, but the respect for everything that Mother Earth offers us and the unconditional love "she" shows us by continually producing enough food and possibilities for us to survive is at least some sort of description.

I also find the Indian way of calling earth Mother and the skies Father sympathetic in its way of making everyone and everything belong to the same family. It makes you view all humans on the planet, as well as all animals and plants as related and that gives you a , completely different feeling than many of the religions do today. The spiritual love has, for me, nothing to do with formalized religion and religious dogmas. If we want to create our own rituals that help us get into the mood there's nothing wrong with that, as long as we use them for our own purposes and don't try to force them on others. As soon as musts and shoulds enter the picture, love atrophies and this is why the religions don't work so smoothly.

If it was the spiritual love that was the source of all religions it's in many cases fear that keep them going. When we look a little closer at the background of the different religions and religious systems of today we find that they all seem to have the same message. It is about love, to be love and do love and that the highest power, no matter what we call it, is love. We cannot blame this love for all the misery that has followed in the steps of religious fanatics' activities, that responsibility lies with human interpretations, lack of this very love and hunger for power. The important thing shouldn't be which book, which philosopher, thinker or other spiritual role model who is the "right one" or which interpretation of the basic philosophy that is correct. The important question is whether we can in fact live in love.

How hard can it be to know what love is and what it is not?

You be the judge, we all have it even if we chose to disregard it in our day to day lives. The fact that we need laws and structure to organize a society is one thing, but to let religious beliefs and interpretations rule these laws and structures is as wise as to claim that all Red Sox' fans are God's people and those who chose to not be Red Sox fans will be punished. Spiritual love is nothing that should be forced by using threats and fear. As I see it there is no trust in religion, at least no trust in its followers since so many religions both historically and now are so filled with musts, shoulds and threats of punishments and eternal pain unless we live in accordance with their rules. This is what I refer to when I say that the origin of religion might have been love, but fear is what keeps the frightened masses adherent. No one wants to be condemned, live in sin, go to hell or anything else that is used to intimidate. Religions with all its influence and power has made entire societies live by the detailed interpretations and not the original message of love. In a way religion can be compared to just about any product or service that is marketed primarily by saying "you don't cut it" and then tell people that this or that religion is the solution to that problem. The arguments used are however more often than not a lot more sinister than that.

We have a need for a feeling of brotherhood of man, to find our "flock" so that we feel that we are connected to others. Unfortunately many groups or such flocks are more a way of excluding others than to be grateful for the community. We create a "them and us", as if one interest or a religion has to be put against something else. Sometimes a war can start just because we disagree about whom is right or we fight to defend our interests or our religion. That's when we have strayed too far away from the basic need of the communal feeling where love rules. In the best of worlds our interests or our specific way to practice our spiritual love wouldn't be mixed in with politics and society's laws and rules. The most important thing is to keep love in focus and not fear. So far, no one could say, that we despite our good intentions, have succeeded. There are daily proofs of this in religious wars, arguments between supporters of different sports clubs, between racists and immigrants, between heterosexuals and homosexuals and the list goes on. This proves that we have distanced ourselves from love, which is accepting and inclusive, and turned to fear which separates and is aggressive.

I'm not saying that we can't have different opinions or not discuss and speak up for ourselves, but there are always better ways to solve an argument than to maim or even kill the opponent. How important is it really if the Bears beat the 49ers, is it really a serious problem, is someone's life dependent on it? When we say that love should be the focus, it's not saying that we always have to be so meek and humble that we turn into doormats. There is a middle ground, but that takes wise and consciously aware people, so that we can calm down and put things in its right perspective.

As I see it, and I may be "new agey", spiritual love, or the love of it all, is free from rules and rigid structures. When we use love as a fundament we are always on the right path. The easiest way to know if we stand on love or fear is to be aware of our feelings inside; if we feel calm, balanced and comfortable when we say or do something we are most likely acting out of love, and if we feel tense, worried or put up resistance we have taken a step over to fear.

Sometimes we seem extremely grim when we talk about religious practices or spirituality, but I'm sure that even God, if she exists, has a sense of humour, since true love and a good sense of humour have so many things in common. Claud Roy, a Canadian author put this brilliantly:

"Love is an attachment to another self. Humour is a form of self-detachment -- a way of looking at one's existence, one's misfortune, or one's discomfort. If you really love, if you really know how to laugh, the result is the same: you forget yourself."

When we allow love to be our foundation, when we give in to our feelings, may it be the love for a romantic partner, our kids, football team or to life itself it is an experience of becoming one with love. We forget our limitations and our limited beliefs for a while and that feels bigger and more powerful than anything we could have imagined. Those moments offer us an experience of how immense love and life truly are.

SEX, PORN AND LOVE

As I'm sure no one has missed, I feel that we have lost sight of love today. We talk too much about sex, but the talking revolves more about techniques, aids and deviant pleasures than about love and all the emotions that are an integral part of sex when at its best. I am convinced that all of us could figure out how to have sex, without any assistance from formal sexual education. It's easy to notice that in nature, all animals know exactly what to do, and they haven't been in any sex education classes. The thing is we don't settle for just reproductive sex, we want a great, inspiring, exciting and fabulous sex life and we want to be the ones deciding whether it should result in children or not. Of course it's a good thing that both sexes have informed each other about how our respective bodies function. But the fact is, that you won't become a great lover just because you've had a lot of sex partners, nor will you accomplish that by learning how to handle a mix of sex toys or aids or because you've studied anatomy. You become a great lover if you're skilled at love.

What does it take to get skilled at love? Well, if you love someone, you give them your full attention. You observe and register all nuances, everything that can tell you what he or she likes and prefers. You approach your loved one with tenderness, warmth, generosity, acceptance and benevolence just because you feel this love and want to offer him or her everything under the moon. When you are truly attentive to someone they feel appreciated and loved and those are the feelings a great lover leaves behind.

189

We speak a lot about the difference of the sexes – I think it was Dr Phil who said that men are more visual and get turned on by images to a higher degree than women, and that women could view something like her man taking out the garbage as a part of a fore-play. That might be to over-simplify it a bit, but yes there are differences in our sex drives. Biologically we know how it works in the animal kingdom and we also have those instincts even if we don't want to view ourselves as animals anymore. It's also a matter of practicality that a female carrying her offspring needs to prioritize differently from a male. No matter how far we develop, this type of instinct will remain and if used properly gives us an understanding of the instinctual needs for the sexes without having to reduce ourselves to or see that as the only explanation or excuse for a dull and uninteresting sex life.

I've heard several men resignedly sigh:*"Women are impossible to understand, what do they want, really?!?!? You are supposed to behave both gently and all sensitive but also be strong and determined or even behave like a classical "bad boy" at times, why is that"?*

How hard can it be? A woman, just like a man, wants variation and besides, the one does not necessarily take out the other. Or wouldn't it be possible to be emotionally present and still be forceful? In principle you could say that the female passion, lust and sex drive are more complex than the male equivalents and grow as a result of a number of factors having to be present simultaneously. These factors include things such as feelings, emotions, atmosphere, clothes, looks, communication and touch.

The saying that a woman, according to man's highest wishes is to be a housekeeper in the living room, a cook in the kitchen and a whore in the bedroom is not new to anyone. And even if it does prove that men as well as women have complex needs when it relates to a love affair compared to a casual fling it also shows that the primary quality for a man's passion is that she is a whore in the bedroom. The Madonna-whore complex – is the more extreme variant of this – men who cannot see the woman as a complex creature and have to divide females into two groups – some are "dirty" and made for sex while others are wife-material. Presumably this is primarily the type of men who are behind porn since porn is so utterly devoid of love or any other more complex feelings. The weird thing is that most porn enthusiasts want to imply that they are the ones who are sexually liberated! If we want to develop as human beings and if we are earnest in our quest for satisfying sex- and love-lives, it's not going to be thru porn we learn.

In conclusion you could say that it up to now primarily has been women who has learned by and adapted to men's sexuality (sometimes to a ridiculous extent) and that this imbalance is the foundation for a lot of things that do not work in our sex lives and relationships today. I am sure that if a larger number of men showed interest in and wanted to learn more about the complexity of female passion we would see a corresponding number of couples with amazing sex- and love lives.

It does make me happy though that the search on the internet so clearly showed that there is more interest for love than for porn. Not that it proves anything, but still it's a signal that we want to know more about how to love or how to feel loved. A signal that tells us that love is important to us, more important than other things. Maybe it's time to question this superficial life style that has now become the norm. To stop living in desperate attempts to uphold our preferred self image or self illusion and instead dive head on straight into the deep sea of feelings and make sure we get soaked from head to toe and also drink deeply from it. Maybe it is so that feelings are something we should treasure, if not higher, so at the very least just as high, as the intellect since no matter how we look at it; it is when we feel strongly and love deeply we feel most vibrantly alive.

"Life is not measured by the number of breaths we take, but by the moments that take our breath away." Boyd Palmer_

CPSIA information can be obtained at www.ICGtesting.com
Printed in the USA
BVOW010959020113

309623BV00008B/124/P